TWO HUNDRED YEARS OF

North American Indian Art

TWO HUNDRED YEARS OF

North American Indian Art

NORMAN FEDER

PRAEGER PUBLISHERS

NEW YORK · WASHINGTON · LONDON

IN ASSOCIATION WITH THE WHITNEY MUSEUM OF AMERICAN ART

PRAEGER PUBLISHERS
111 Fourth Avenue, New York, N.Y. 10003, U.S.A.
5, Cromwell Place, London SW7 2JL, England
Published in the United States of America in 1971 by Praeger Publishers, Inc.,
in association with the Whitney Museum of American Art
Second printing, 1972
© 1971 by the Whitney Museum of American Art
All rights reserved
Library of Congress Catalog Card Number: 70–176395

Printed in the United States of America

Contents

v

Preface

The art of the North American Indian has long been recognized for its ethnographic importance. It is the most vivid record we have of the economic, social, and religious systems of the diverse tribes that have inhabited this continent. It is therefore not surprising that the earliest and most extensive collections of American Indian art are in scientific museums or specialized institutions for ethnographic studies.

Our awareness of the aesthetic importance of Indian art is much more recent. The modernist revolution of the early twentieth century opened the way to a new understanding of the formal beauty of so-called primitive painting and sculpture, but it did not extend its appreciation to the American Indian culture. Perhaps the first major art museum to do so was the Museum of Modern Art in New York, where René d'Harnoncourt and Frederic H. Douglas organized an exhibition, *Indian Art of the United States,* in 1941, accompanied by a book of the same title. I still recall the revelation it was to all of us, except presumably experts in the field, at that time.

That was thirty years ago. Since then, knowledge of American Indian art has greatly increased and many new objects of high aesthetic quality have come to light. It seemed to us at the Whitney Museum of American Art that the time had come for another comprehensive showing of this most native of all our arts. With the aid of a very generous grant from Philip Morris Incorporated, the exhibition was assembled on which this book is based. It was selected by Norman Feder, Curator of American Indian and Native Arts at The Denver Art Museum, who is also the author of the book.

Wisely, I think, Mr. Feder has chosen to concentrate on the historic period of Indian art. For reasons that he explains, he has not attempted to cover prehistoric or contemporary work. What we have here, then, is that great flowering of tribal arts which constitute the principal and still-living tradition of American Indians. That it has remained so little known is one more proof, if proof be needed, of our extraordinary lack of sensitivity to the high artistic contribution made by the original inhabitants of this continent.

JOHN I. H. BAUR

I.   (preceding page) Clan hat of wood—Tsimshian (Kitkatla, B.C.). 17″ *high;* 12½″ *base diameter. Painted black, red, and green. Mouth contains seashell teeth and bear canines. Collection of the National Museum of Man, National Museums of Canada, Ottawa.*

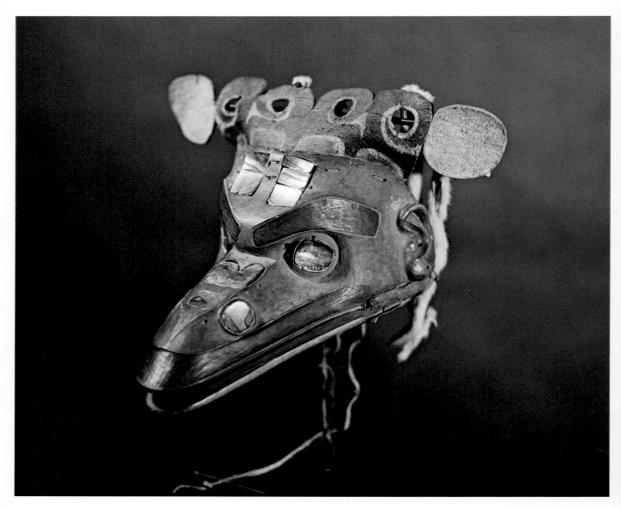

II.   Swan mask—Tlingit-Klukwan. 12″ *long. Abalone-shell inlay with painted leather crown and pendant ermine skins. Movable lower jaw. Collection of Mr. and Mrs. Morton I. Sosland.*

Introduction

When I was approached by the Whitney Museum of American Art to prepare an exhibition and book on American Indian art, my first inclination was to choose the same approach that has been taken over and over in the past; that is, to present a broad spectrum of Indian arts and crafts from the prehistoric through the modern period. However, the more I reflected, the more I was inclined to take advantage of the opportunity to present something more unique. I had long felt that a vast portion of Indian art from the Plains and Woodlands regions was little known and sadly neglected, and that I would like to show the public a little more than it is accustomed to seeing in the ordinary exhibitions and art books. Briefly stated, my purpose is to present the very best American Indian art from the historic period and to include all of North America north of Mexico. I have also tried to select objects that anyone can relate to.

There are several advantages to this approach. The public will be introduced to many forms of Indian art that it was not aware of and undoubtedly will be intrigued by its beauty and variety. Contemporary American Indians will find something that they can relate to, for all of the pieces included derive from historic tribal groups, and not from unidentified prehistoric areas.

Partly because of space limitations and my desire to show more of what I felt were neglected art forms, partly because I wanted to present something a little different, I was forced to limit the content of *Two Hundred Years of North American Indian Art.* First, I have chosen to ignore prehistoric art. My reasons are that prehistoric art is well represented in most of the country's major museum displays as well as in many commonly available art books. To do justice to prehistoric Indian art would require a great deal more space than is available. However, my principal reason was to avoid giving the impression that Indians stopped producing anything worthwhile after white contact; and, conversely, that Indians have produced some truly remarkable works of art during comparatively recent times.

For many reasons, I have also chosen not to include contemporary Indian art. This should in no way imply that contemporary Indian artists are not the equal of, or even superior to, their ancestors. Again, space limitation was important, and I was also influenced by the fact that contemporary Indian artists can exhibit their works at a dozen or more major annual shows. Thus, their works do receive exposure and are considerably better known than the older masterpieces included here. Originally, my intention was to include a few representative examples of both contemporary and prehistoric art, but I decided against this approach: a few items would not be really representative, and I also felt that the selection would be more cohesive and meaningful if I rigidly restricted it to the best art of the historic period up to about 1900. Hopefully, in the near future, someone will organize a major exhibition devoted exclusively to prehistoric art, and another to contemporary art.

An additional limitation is the exclusion of many types of crafts, as opposed to arts. Since I am deeply involved with, and very fond of, all types of Indian arts and crafts, I had to adopt certain arbitrary standards as a safeguard against my own biases. I tried to avoid including pieces simply because they are very old and rare, or extremely good technically, and I have attempted to select only those objects that are of artistic excellence. The latter is perhaps a completely arbitrary limitation reflecting my own personal judgment.

Two Hundred Years of North American Indian Art

Is a specialized background necessary to fully appreciate North American Indian art? What is Indian art, as opposed to Indian crafts? Who produced the art, and why? What materials and techniques were employed in its production? These are some of the questions I hope to answer in this brief survey.

Many writers on the subject of American Indian art are under the mistaken impression that, for the viewer to really appreciate Indian art, he must try to look at it as an Indian would. This is the equivalent of saying that a person would have to be an ancient Greek to understand ancient Greek art. While it is certainly true that a Sioux Indian born and brought up on a Sioux reservation will have a different view of Sioux art than a non-Indian, it is also true that his impressions will be different from any non-Sioux Indian. Likewise, the fact that he is a Sioux will not give him special insights into the art of any other tribe. Furthermore, his tastes will be far different from those of his father and grandfather because ideas of beauty vary from time to time and from place to place. The introduction of new materials, for example, almost always causes changes in arts and crafts. Indians were quick to accept brightly colored beads, silk ribbons, and aniline dyes to replace the more pastel colors of native pigments. Indians today will often go to great trouble and expense to repaint an old mask or totem pole with bright commercial house paints because, to them, the newer and brighter the object looks, the more beautiful it is. To the Indian, a mask, blanket, basket, or a pot is something to be used, and it should not look dull and worn. This is somewhat similar to a modern-day housewife dying a faded dress or a man polishing a pair of shoes. Yet, the average collector, museum curator, and Indian art expert bemoans the fact that an old mask is repainted, or that Navaho are using aniline dyes in their rugs instead of the softer native vegetable dyes of a bygone day. It seems that we are not only incapable of looking at Indian art as an Indian would, but that we really do not want to, preferring instead to gaze at it romantically.

My contention is that anyone can appreciate American Indian art regardless of his knowledge, background, or previous experience. Anyone glancing through the photographs in this book or looking at the objects on display will most certainly find some things he considers attractive or appealing. Several investigators have proved that there are certain universal ideals of beauty.[1] But there is also the matter of individual taste, which is not universal in a complex society like ours. Rarity, age, romantic appeal, and what other people have told us about a particular art are just a few of the factors that affect our ideals of beauty. While I do not expect everyone to like all of the items included here as much as I do, I hope that each person will find at least a few things truly delightful.

THE INDIAN ARTIST

With the possible exception of the Pacific Northwest Coast, to the Indian there were no artists, only craftsmen, some better than others. Each family unit was self-sufficient and able to produce all the essentials of life. In the Southwest, every Pueblo woman made her own pottery; on the Plains, every woman tanned her own skins and sewed all of her family's clothes. Technical skill was everywhere valued and some craftsmen were well known for their pottery or beadwork. The craftworker took great pride in his skill and reveled in the high regard that his tribe accorded him. Industriousness was also applauded to the point where women would boast about how many tipi linings they had beaded or buffalo robes they had tanned. Each craftworker strove for technical proficiency and high productivity, with less emphasis on artistic inventiveness. In fact, the craftworker was allowed very little freedom of expression, since standards of taste were defined within very strict limits. Because of this rigid adherence to traditional use of color, design, and technique, it is possible for an expert to distinguish a pair of Cheyenne moccasins from a pair made by a Sioux; or a water jar made at Santo Domingo from one made at Santa Clara. Further, the factor of ethnocentrism is so important that a Sioux, accustomed to the color and design on traditional Sioux moccasins, would find a pair of Cheyenne moccasins unattractive, even though he perhaps might appreciate the technical proficiency involved in the manufacture.

Some craftwork was cherished more for its prestige value than for its technical excellence. This holds true for objects made from rare and costly materials. Examples are the use of red coral, spiny oyster shell, and turquoise in the Southwest, or of dentalium shells on the Plains. When glass beads were first introduced on the Plains by fur traders, they were expensive, available in limited supply and in only a few colors. Therefore, any object decorated with glass beads was a prestige item, worn not only with pride, but also considered beautiful. When imported woolen cloth was first introduced in the trade, it had the same sort of impact, and anyone who could afford to purchase the material would use it instead of the hand-tanned buckskins. In recent years, with fewer and fewer women tanning hides, the reverse is true: anyone can go to the local store and buy all the cloth he wants, but few can afford the expensive skins.

When a family wanted its newly made tipi or tipi lining decorated with painted pictographic war-exploit drawings, it would not seek out the warrior with the best painting skills but the one with the best war record. Here again, prestige takes precedence over technical excellence.

It is in the realm of religion that we find a higher degree of specialization between the roles of artist and craftsman, and a wider latitude of inventiveness in design. Religious concepts along with the accompanying paraphernalia often originate in hallucinatory visions and because of this do not have to confrom so rigidly to culturally defined norms. In practice, however, only the exceptional visionary will hallucinate beyond the accepted traditional limits. The practice of each individual (usually male) to seek some sort of spiritual helper through a visionary quest is fairly widespread but not universal throughout the Indian tribes of the United States and Canada. The concept seems to be that life on this earth is difficult at best, and that to be successful (in love, war, hunting, health) one needs some sort of spiritual assistance. On the Plains, the standard procedure is for a youth to go off alone for a period of three or four days, usually to a distant mountain top. There he prays, fasts, and sometimes indulges in self-torture (so that the spirits will take pity on him), to the point where fatigue induces a vision. In the usual vision, an animal (real or imaginary), plant, or inanimate object appears to the visionary with instructions that may determine the individual's role within his society for the rest of his life. He may be told to avoid certain foods, to devote his life to the healing arts, to become a great warrior, to marry five wives, and so on. He may also be given a number of instructions concerning charms he should wear, a design to paint on his shield, a song to sing; or in rare instances, the introduction of a new religion complete with songs, dances, rituals, and equipment. The vision of the Sioux woman who started the Dream Dance (or Drum) religion is one example of this phenomenon. Her vision came to her while she was forced to remain for several days partly submerged in water, without food, to escape detection by a group of soldiers.[2] Throughout the Coast Salish area of upper Washington and southern British Columbia, the dominant religious theme was for each person to acquire a personal spirit helper who would stay with him throughout his life. In southern California, jimsonweed (*Datura*) was used to help induce visions among young boys undergoing a puberty ceremony.

The main point here is that religious art is often a little more complex, original, made with greater attention to detail, and frequently more forceful than ordinary domestic art, and as such, usually has a greater emotional appeal for the average viewer. It is not surprising, then, to find that the majority of items illustrated here were originally intended for religious use. Compare, for example, secular with church art of the Gothic and early Renaissance periods in Europe.

Under the same general heading of religious art, we also find the art produced by the individual shaman (medicine man or doctor). The shaman secures his power through visions and usually manufactures all of his own equipment. In time, if the shaman is particularly effective, he may gather together a group of followers and imitators who will eventually form a new religion or healing society. The Medewiwin (Grand Medicine Lodge) among some Great Lakes tribes supposedly began this way, and most likely the groups of Bear Doctors among some Pueblo tribes had similar origins.

If a distinction can be made between the artist and the craftsman, it is perhaps that the real artist is the visionary, the dreamer, the founder of new religions. Artists are people who are inventive, imaginative, and creative, who reach beyond the limits imposed by their culture and produce new art forms. Of course, once the new form becomes established it, too, becomes traditionally defined. Then we find that some craftsmen become more capable of producing in the new form than others; in other words, they become better technicians.

The Pacific Northwest Coast area from Yakutat south to the Nootka areas of southern British Columbia presents a somewhat different art orientation. Here, too, the individual shaman receives his powers from visions, and shamanistic art constitutes some of the most powerful art on the coast. The difference is that the carving of vast quantities of masks, headdresses, totem poles, and house posts was restricted to a limited number of professionals. These specialists received formal training through an apprenticeship system, and they were ranked according to their ability. A carver with a good reputation could command a certain price for his services. Northwest Coast culture could be defined simply as an almost constant pursuit of prestige through a system of giving lavish feasts, or potlatches, to validate a claim to an inherited prerogative. These prerogatives included the right to perform certain dances and to use certain animal crests, the right to build a certain type of house or to use certain titles and names. When a Northwest Coast Indian of high position wanted to build a house or to erect a totem pole, he would hire the best carver and pay as much as he could afford. However, proper protocol required that the carver not be a direct relation, but rather a member of another clan. The value of the house or totem pole, from the standpoint of prestige, would be in direct relation to the cost involved, in both its production and dedication. Often the fee to the carver would be a small part of the total cost involved in erecting the pole and giving the necessary feasts to validate the prerogative and pay all the attending witnesses. Obviously, then, to a Northwest Coast Indian, it is possible that a small, poorly carved pole could be more important than a large, finely carved one, if the smaller pole involved a higher cost.

Still another facet of the role of the artist involves the process of acculturation. For at least 150 years and possibly longer, there has been a series of new, innovative forms developed by American Indians solely to meet the demands of a developing tourist industry. From the early 1800's, tourists came in flocks to visit Niagara Falls and the Falls of Saint Anthony. Later, they took the tour boats to Alaska and the trains to Santa Fe. One impetus for the development of new art forms was the desire to gain a larger share of the tourist dollar. Some of the art produced for tourist sale was merely a degenerate form of traditional art altered for non-Indian taste. However, other kinds of art were devoid of tradition, such as the Haida's use of argillite, at first for carving copies of whaler's scrimshaw and later for producing miniature totem poles and carved chests in the new material. Still other innovations include the development of several new pottery types at San Juan, Santa Clara, and San Ildefonso; the concept of watercolor paintings on paper; and the elaboration of jewelry and rug production in the Southwest, some of which was instigated by non-Indians.

The businessmen who ran the Indian trading posts had a financial interest in the sale of Indian crafts. The more they sold, the more money they made. The traders could control craft production by buying only the items they liked and could easily resell, or by refusing to purchase other items. Depending on the time, place, and the type of trader, this could have the effect of insuring a high degree of technical excellence (as with the Navaho Arts and Crafts Guild); of encouraging shoddy workmanship (as among some of the traders in the Gallup, New Mexico, area who developed an inexpensive product known as the Gallup Throw Rug); or even of introducing totally new design forms (like the so-called Crystal pattern rug developed by a trader named Moore at the Crystal Trading Post). The point that must be made here is that, in general, Indians were not lacking in the ability to be innovative and creative, given the proper motivation, but rather, they were restricted by the limits imposed by their society.

THE FUNCTION OF ART

To the American Indian, everything he made had a function. The idea of hanging a painting on a wall or placing a sculpture on a pedestal, just to admire it, was completely alien to him. Man everywhere seems to enjoy having beautiful things about him, and the American Indian was no exception. Almost everything was decorated in some way, although some things were more lavishly designed than others. It always took a little more time to decorate an object that would have been just as useful if left alone, but if the time was available, the object usually received some kind of elaboration simply to make it more attractive. We would thus expect to find more profuse and elaborate decorations in a society with more leisure time, and of course, this is the case. Indians living in the Great Basin areas of Utah and Nevada had almost no time to spare apart from the daily struggle of securing a livelihood, and so they produced little in the way of decorative art. In contrast, the Indians living on the Pacific Northwest Coast had an abundant supply of fish, and so had ample time to decorate nearly everything they used.

The Indians of the Plains region usually had enough food from the buffalo herds (particularly after the introduction of the horse), but because of their nomadic life, they were forced to limit their artistic production to items that could be easily carried from place to place. The objects the Plains Indians deemed most worthy of transport were, of course, the ones necessary for survival: food, clothing, shelter, eating utensils, hunting equipment, and the tools needed for skin preparation. Equally important were the items connected with ceremonial usage—the various protective medicines of war, such as painted shields, war clubs, and medicine bundles. Also of value were the various accouterments of the many military and age-grade societies. Before the introduction of the horse on the Plains, the Indians had to carry everything they owned on their backs or strapped to their dogs. The horse increased their mobility, allowed them to follow the buffalo herds more easily, and enabled them to transport material possessions and luxury items. Most of the luxury items (things like glass mirrors, metal utensils, and silver jewelry) were supplied by the traders.

Why are some objects left undecorated, some just slightly ornamented, and others elaborately embellished? There is no one answer to this question, but we can give a few specific reasons. Items that tend to break easily or are made for a one-time use generally tend to receive little decoration. This group would include such things as animal traps, temporary shelters, or ceramics used by nomadic peoples. Generally, clothing designed for everyday use is left largely undecorated. Soft-soled moccasins wear out quickly, particularly the ones worn by men on hunting or war journeys, so it would be foolish to spend time decorating a short-lived article. In contrast, clothing designed for important functions is always decorated with as much care as skill and time will allow. From the Plains east, it was a matter of great pride for a woman to dress her husband in the finest garments possible. Of course, the husband had to supply the raw materials (beads, skins, cloth) and the wife had to do all the hide-tanning, bead-sewing, and so on, to put it all together.

One reason for elaborate decoration was related to the widespread custom of gift-giving. Items manufactured as gifts almost always were produced with special care, so that the maker could show his high regard for the recipient. Such items as sewing awls and heddles for bead-weaving were made by the men as gifts to their female relatives. The same is true of the spindle whorls used by Cowichan women to spin their yarn. On the Plains, a new-born baby might receive up to a half dozen fully beaded cradle boards as gifts from admiring sisters and aunts. Among the Hopi, the men made and decorated the elaborate tablita (headdress) worn by their female partners in the Butterfly Dance. Most tribes had at least one organized give-a-way festival, something like the potlatch on the Northwest Coast. Among the Eskimo, it was the Messenger Feast; on the Plains, it was often known as a Pony Smoke, which was incorporated into the Grass Dance. All major Woodland Indian ceremonies featured large feasts as part of the rite, and the so-called Adoption Dance, or Shawnee Dance, included the lavish giving of gifts. Prestige depended on giving as much as possible in both quantity and quality. However, sometimes the feasts took the form of a "potluck" dinner in which everyone contributed to the best of his ability, a wealthy person supplying the meat and the poorer people collecting wild plants.

Kachina is the generic name for the deities of the Pueblo Indians in New Mexico and Arizona. During ceremonies throughout the year, the men don masks and impersonate the gods in dance and ritual to bring rain, insure good crops, and ward off illness in their villages. Small versions of the Kachina dancers, known as Kachina dolls, are carved in wood and presented to the children, who play with them and hang them in their homes. The dolls thus serve as an educational toy, in that the children, while playing, learn about their gods.

Besides prestige, vanity was a principal factor determining the amount of decoration. Everywhere people wanted to dress in beautiful garments. Men kept their wives and female relatives busy manufacturing clothing, and they also produced and purchased a good deal of what they wore themselves. Early travelers on the Plains sometimes gave the impression that the average male spent all of his time applying makeup, combing his hair, and donning his best clothing and jewelry. His vanity even carried over to elaborate decorations for his horse, and to objects carried in secular dances, such as fancifully carved mirror frames.

Related to vanity and prestige as important aspects of motivation for decoration is pride in craftsmanship. If a man flaunts his beautiful garments, his wife and other relatives gain in prestige because of their ability to make the various items. In the Southwest, Pueblo potters vie with one another to see who can make the thinnest and best-decorated pottery; again, pride in craftsmanship is related to prestige. The same is true of craftsmen everywhere. A true craftsman will not hurry or produce poor work even under economic pressure. There are today craftworkers in silver, carving, basketry, and ceramics in many parts of the country who still refuse to produce poor-quality work, even though they know that their things will be sold to tourists who, in many cases, will not appreciate the technical skill that went into the production.

The main factor in determining what will be decorated, and to what extent the decorations will be applied, is linked directly to religious practices. A comparison of items made for secular use with those designed for sacred use makes this immediately apparent. The smoking of tobacco, usually mixed with one or more other plants and known as kinnikinnick, was a widespread custom over much of the country. Smoking pipes designed for secular, that is, everyday use, are usually simply made and without elaboration. On the other hand, tobacco was considered a sacred plant over much of the Plains and Woodland areas, and smoking was an activity associated with all important religious ceremonies. Pipes designed for religious use were always profusely decorated, sometimes in a prescribed manner. The pipe bowls were made of soft stone (the preferred material was often catlinite, also called pipestone, mainly from quarries near the town of Pipestone, Minnesota), and they usually had detailed carvings of human or animal forms. The long wooden stems used with these pipe bowls were also decorated with carvings or applied porcupine-quill work. In addition, entire ceremonial complexes developed around the planting and harvesting of the tobacco crop, even among tribal groups who practiced no other agriculture. The Crow tribe, for example, developed specially painted clothing and special medicine bundles, all related to the planting of tobacco.[3]

A similar comparison can be made between the wooden spoons and bowls used from the East Coast to the Eastern Plains. Spoons and bowls designed for everyday use were often of soft woods carved very simply. In contrast, those designed for the Grand Medicine Lodge ceremonies, the Dream Dance religion, and other important religious functions were often made from hard tree burls and decorated with human or animal forms. Occasionally, spoons and bowls in everyday use were also made from decorated burls, but the tendency was always toward more elaborate decoration on sacred items.

The most inventive artistic products produced by American Indians are the religious articles that have no secular prototype. These are the vision-inspired objects developed solely for religious purposes. The masks of the Alaskan Eskimo, in an infinite variety of form, are among the most imaginative art produced anywhere in the world.[4] Considering that the masks were produced by a relatively homogeneous group of people living in a fairly small area of coastal Alaska, the diversity of fanciful forms is truly staggering. Needless to say, the masks are conceived by shamans as a visionary experience. The typical vision consists of the Eskimo shaman's traveling great distances to the spirit world, sometimes over land, sometimes under water, or even to the sun or moon. The resulting masks are often extremely powerful because of their purposeful distortions.

As part of my duties at the Denver Art Museum, I often give seminars on African art to groups of art students. One of the things I frequently ask the students to do is to experiment with a lump of clay and produce variations on the human face by intentional distortion. I encourage the students to let their imaginations run wild—to extend a nose, diminish an eye, or misshape an ear. Then during the course of the seminar, we look at African masks and marvel at the fact that African artists produced almost every distortion that we could imagine. It is a rare occasion when a student comes up with a totally new idea. The point I want to make here is that the Alaskan Eskimo, occupying a much smaller land area, has developed almost as much imaginative distortion as all of Africa. Eskimo carving (particularly masking) is certainly a neglected art form. There are very few publications on traditional Eskimo art compared to the vast literature on African art, and as far as I know, there has never been a comprehensive exhibit of Eskimo masks.

I have already discussed several kinds of vision-induced art, such as the Dream Dance and its specially decorated drum and ritual, but there are also a few other interesting forms. On the Pacific Northwest Coast, particularly among the northern groups—the Tlingit, Tsimshian, and Haida—the shaman was mainly responsible for dealing with illness. Each shaman had one or more visions that gave him the power to heal or sometimes to locate missing objects or even to foretell the future. His visions gave him the proper ritual and song as well as the specific form of rattle, headdress, ivory charm, and painting on drum or kilt. Some of these shaman masks, maskettes, and charms are among the best work produced in the area. Further south, among Salish-speaking people, the particular form of a wand, dancing stick, or mask was also revealed to the owner in a vision, but here, almost everyone had a vision in which a personal spirit helper appeared.

Throughout the Plains, visions were eagerly sought through special vision quests. Designs painted on shields were obtained from visions, but sometimes if a man was not fortunate in securing a successful vision of his own, he could purchase the protective power, including the use of a shield design, of someone else's vision. The two paintings on paper illustrated in this catalogue show the dream of the blacktail deer, a common dream occurrence among the Sioux, where everyone with a similar dream experience would band together to form a society. Individual visions were also responsible for the painted robes of the Arapaho and Crow. Visions on parts of the Plains area were a fairly common experience and usually resulted in the visionary's making up a medicine bundle, which consisted of objects seen in the vision. Medicine bundles took a great variety of forms[5] and were not always as artistic as the war shields. The typical bundle was a collection of feathers, stones, animal parts, and so on, all placed in a skin container.

Among the Iroquois Indians of upper New York State and sections of Canada, carved wooden masks seem to be part of an ancient custom. Masks are used mainly in a curing ceremony whose origins are told in mythology. The custom is for any man who dreams of a False Face to thereupon join the Masked Medicine Society; however, members are also recruited among people who have been cured by society rites. The masks are of infinite variety, within a series of prescribed limits, because the particular form is determined by the person's dream experience. The members of the society wear their masks during an annual ceremony to cleanse the village of evil and sickness, and at any other time they are called upon to effect a cure. At one time, these masks were carved into a living tree with the proper ritual of prayer and burning tobacco. Today this is no longer done. Many Iroquois groups still use the masks as an active part of their ceremonies, but a few professional carvers are producing them in large numbers for sale.[6]

A form of masking was once practiced by the Delaware Indians, who were neighbors to the Iroquois on the East Coast. The Delaware were displaced, however, at an early date and moved about the country from Canada to Oklahoma under pressures of both Indians and non-Indians. Somewhere along the way, they lost their masking complex. The small group of Delaware Indians who eventually settled in the vicinity of Dewey, Copan, and Wann, Oklahoma, remained a little more conservative than most of the other small remnant groups. The carved faces illustrated here were on supporting posts of a ceremonial Big House, which was still standing near Copan in 1910.[7]

The Cherokee Indians in the Great Smoky Mountains near the town of Cherokee, North Carolina, have also developed a secular masking complex, but it is believed to be a fairly recent development, with little or no basis in tradition.

Artistic production survived as long as it continued to serve a function within the society. The tremendous influx of Europeans into North America had a far-reaching impact on native Indian cultures. It caused a series of displacements in which Indians moved from their age-old environments to new lands. Some tribes like the Kickapoo were so scattered after a series of moves, that groups of Kickapoo, who originally lived in Wisconsin, then moved to Missouri and Texas, now occupy land in Michigan, Kansas, Oklahoma, and Mexico. Their cultures were forced to change somewhat in their new environments because of new materials, cultural interchange with other Indian groups encountered along the way, and the influence of non-Indians. In Illinois and Kansas, they were introduced to Christianity and some were converted to the new religion. One Kickapoo visionary named Kenakuk introduced a new religion based partly on a Christian model. There are still approximately two hundred Kickapoo who follow the Kenakuk religion in Kansas.[8] Other Kansas Kickapoo are devout Christians, others are followers of the Dream Dance (Drum) religion, and still others are members of the Native American Church (the Peyote religion). Today none of the Kansas Kickapoo follow the teachings of the Grand Medicine Lodge (Medewiwin), which was the dominant religion of these people when they lived in Wisconsin. It should be easy to see that, with the decay of old religions, the paraphernalia of sacred rituals ceased to serve a valid function within the society and are consequently no longer made. This would include such items as the juggler dolls, which were employed to produce magical tricks as a part of the Grand Medicine Lodge ceremonies. Of course, the new religions needed new forms of ritual equipment. The Dream Dance not only called for the use of specially decorated drums, but also required special smoking pipes with stems and wooden bowls—a direct transfer from the older Grand Medicine Lodge equipment. The Kenakuk Church developed a special form of wooden prayer stick that was carried by each member; and the Native American Church introduced a series of new ritual equipment consisting of specially constructed gourd rattles, feather fans, decorated staffs, water drums, and a wide variety of jewelry and insignia.

The Native American Church, also known as the Peyote religion, is probably the dominant Indian religion in the United States today. It is comparatively new, having become popular in southern Oklahoma among the

Kiowa and Comanche eighty to ninety years ago. Today it is practiced by most tribal groups in Oklahoma and is very popular among such scattered tribes as the Winnebago in Wisconsin and the Navaho in Arizona. The trend seems to be that when it becomes the dominant religion, it either completely replaces the older forms of religious art or greatly diminishes them.

One of the major reasons for the breakdown of the traditional religious activities of many tribal groups is that the changes brought about by acculturation eliminated the need for the old concepts. On the Plains after the 1860's, when the Indians were placed on reservations, they lost the need for protective war medicines and hunting charms. Warfare was completely eliminated and hunting became a minor activity in comparison to the major role it had played in pre-reservation days. The vision quest became less important, shields and war clubs were no longer needed, and military societies were disbanded because they no longer served a useful function. The effect of placing a nomadic, warrior, hunting people on a confined reservation was quite debilitating. By 1890, they received word of a new religion called the Ghost Dance, developed in a vision by a Paiute Indian named Wovoka, from Walker Lake, Nevada. The Ghost Dance predicted that the white man would disappear, the buffalo would return, and that long-deceased ancestors would return to a heaven on earth. It spread over much of the Plains area but faded quickly because none of the promises materialized. Among the Rosebud Sioux at Wounded Knee, South Dakota, it led to a massacre of Indians by white soldiers, apparently because the Indian agent at the time thought the Indians were gathering for military reasons. Even though the religion was short-lived, it had a long-lasting effect on art as well as songs and dances. Specially painted shirts and dresses were made to be worn during the Ghost Dance ceremonies. These garments were said to be magically endowed to ward off the white man's bullets. A special form of the "hand game" (a guessing game involving gambling), complete with songs and equipment, accompanied the spread of the Ghost Dance ceremonies.

In the Southwest, the Pueblo Indians were placed in direct contact with Spanish-speaking peoples from as early as 1540, when Coronado came from Mexico searching for gold. Shortly after, other people made the same northward trek from Mexico, including missionaries who hoped to convert the Indians to Catholicism, and others who simply were seeking a place to farm in an unsettled area. The missionaries succeeded in establishing a church at each pueblo. Although many of the Indians embraced Catholicism, they never gave up their older, established religions. It was almost as if they felt, if one religion is good, two are better. However, they did object to the alien intruders on their lands, and in 1680 the Pueblos banded together and expelled all of the Spaniards from New

Mexico, killing most of the priests and burning many of the churches. The Spanish returned by 1692 and have been there since; but the Pueblos do not give up their traditions easily, and most have managed to retain a substantial part of their original culture.

In other areas of the United States, the Indians did not fare so well. The same process of Spanish colonization and missionary zeal occurred in southern California, but there the Indians were partly wiped out by disease, partly assimilated, so that today only a few Indian groups remain, and they have kept little of their original culture. In parts of the Southeast, the so-called five civilized tribes—Cherokee, Choctaw, Creek, Chickasaw, and Seminole—seemed to welcome the white intruders and to imitate their ways. Some groups like the Cherokee underwent a rapid acculturation process, and as early as 1828 were publishing their own newspaper. They adopted Christianity, built libraries and universities, and in general lost most of their Indian heritage.

It seems inevitable that whenever two groups with different cultural backgrounds mingle, either on a voluntary or an involuntary basis, a gradual process of assimilation occurs. Each loses part of its own heritage and gains part of the culture of the other group. The dominant group will tend to lose less and, possibly, gain more; the reverse is also true. American Indians are a minority in the United States and Canada, and it thus seems inevitable that eventually they will be assimilated completely. But the process is fortunately slow, and it is slower among some groups than others. The Cherokee apparently welcomed assimilation, while the Pueblo groups are still fighting it. Tribes from the eastern seaboard, which have been in contact with Europeans since the 1500's, have rarely retained much of their culture, but again, some have been able to keep more than others. Most eastern groups were removed to portions of the West; the small remnant groups that still live on reservations in the New England area would probably not be recognized as Indians by the average visitor. The Iroquois of upper New York State and Canada are an exception in that they seem to have held on to a good portion of their traditions, or "Indianness." Yet the dominant Iroquois religion is the Code of Handsome Lake, which was initiated by a Seneca prophet named Handsome Lake around 1799.

Very little of the art of southern California, the southeastern states, or the Atlantic seaboard is illustrated here simply because only a small part of the art from the historic period remains. There are wonderful collections of prehistoric art from these areas, and undoubtedly great art continued to be produced during the early historic period, but what little of it was collected has long since been lost. Early historic collections were not well cared for in the sense that there were no museums to house them: the first American museum was established in Charleston, South Carolina, in 1773; but the oldest museum still in operation is the Peabody Museum in Salem, Massachusetts, which opened in 1779.[9] During the later historic period, of the past 270 years or so, the Indians of most of these areas have been so acculturated that little in the way of traditional art forms were produced.

One final illustration of how an art form disappears once it no longer serves a valid function within society, can be found in the art of the Pacific Northwest Coast. In the Northwest Coast culture, with its emphasis on gaining prestige, there was an almost continual demand for new art products in the form of totem poles, house posts, grave markers, masks, shamanistic equipment, clothing, boxes, and household utensils. A visit to the storerooms of one of our museums with major collections of Indian art, such as the Field Museum in Chicago, The American Museum of Natural History in New York, the National Museum of Man in Ottawa, or the Provincial Museum in Victoria, would convince anyone that the quantity of production was truly staggering. The impact of the white man on the Northwest Coast tended to increase rather than diminish this supply. The white man not only introduced more and better metal tools, but he also brought increased wealth, which had the effect of stimulating the potlatch system. While this kind of acceleration was in progress, a deceleration began as the result of new diseases and a disruption of the established community and clan relationships. Entire villages were abandoned and the people moved to new locations in order to be closer to a cannery, school, hospital, or trading post. In addition, some white communities such as Sitka, Alaska,were established directly on the site of an Indian village simply because the Indians had picked the best beach location.

These changes in the economy and settlement patterns gradually brought about the inevitable acculturation. Thus, throughout most of the northern part of the Pacific coast, the entire system of potlatching was practically nonexistent by 1900. Farther south, the Indian Act of British Columbia outlawed the potlatch in 1921. Violators, when caught, were fined, imprisoned, and their ritual equipment frequently confiscated. The law of 1921 was not the sole cause of the demise of the potlatch system, for groups like the Kwakiutl did continue to potlatch in remote villages. When the law was repealed (by being left out of the 1951 Indian Act), the potlatch again flourished in a small revival. Today the Kwakiutl still have an occasional potlatch, but for all practical purposes the system is dead. Because the potlatch continued as a living idea among the Kwakiutl, and to a lesser extent among the Tsimshian, these tribes still have several craftsmen trained as carvers in the old apprenticeship system. In recent years, there have also been training programs to produce even more artists, and since the demand by tourists and museums for good carving has increased, the supply is also increasing in both quantity and quality. Probably the most successful recent project of this type is at Hazelton, British Columbia, where the Tsimshian have established a museum of older tribal arts, a reconstructed village, workshops, and a craft sales outlet.[10] It should now be clear from this discussion that there has been a series of changes in the amount and quality of artistic production since the time of first white contact. Today, art is still being made, but the reasons for it are different. Art no longer serves a traditional function in Northwest Coast culture; rather, it is a source of income and manufactured almost entirely for its sale value.

MATERIALS AND TECHNIQUES

In general, Indians everywhere have always used whatever materials have been available; that is, they exploited their environment to the best of their ability. In forested regions such as the Pacific Northwest Coast and the Woodlands, Indians naturally made much use of forest products. Northwest Coast Indians made from wood homes, food and storage containers, boats, as well as masks, totem poles, and grave markers. Woodland peoples used wood for spoons and bowls, and bark to cover their homes (either elm or birch bark, depending on the area). In the Plains, where buffalo were abundant and trees scarce, the popular tipi was developed as a skin-covered structure, spoons were made of buffalo horns, and even paintbrushes were made of porous buffalo bones. In the Southwest, pottery and basketry were common, and wood was used for only a small number of products, such as Kachina dolls. Wherever soapstone or catlinite was found, it was used for smoking pipes and cooking bowls. Large sheep horns were made into eating bowls in areas where mountain sheep roamed; and everywhere feathers, dye plants, animal or vegetable fibers for cordage and weaving, and items such as porcupine quills and moose hair for embroidery, were employed.

Because of the emphasis on prestige, uncommon types of materials were eagerly sought, and a vast intertribal trade developed in these items. Catlinite from the Minnesota quarries was traded all the way to the state of Washington for use in making pipes. Abalone shells from the West Coast could be found in the Plains area, along with a limited supply of dentalium shells. Cast metal bells from the Valley of Mexico were traded in the Pueblo regions of New Mexico and Arizona in return for turquoise. Intertribal trade, usually underestimated, was really quite active and extensive. Invariably, the first white explorers in a new area found that the materials of the white fur trade had preceded them. Indians were often using the white man's beads, metal knives, silver jewelry, and cloth products before they ever met their first trader. However, the quantities they had received were small, and they were eager to obtain more. This led to the development of a large fur-trade industry, with trading posts appearing all over the country. The fur traders blazed the way for future travelers and later settlers; they also disrupted traditional settlement and subsistence patterns, which paved the way for acculturation. The fur trade often proved extremely lucrative for people such as John Jacob Astor, who built a monopoly that controlled a large area of the country. In Canada, the Hudson's Bay Company did much the same thing, literally forcing its competitors out of business.

Indian technology was limited, partly from an absence of raw materials, partly from a lack of knowledge as to how to use the materials available. North of Mexico, the science of metallurgy was practically nonexistent; only native copper found in pure nugget form was employed. Copper was used in Wisconsin in prehistoric times, and in parts of Alaska and elsewhere, but it was never abundant and it did not serve well for the manufacture of cutting tools. Likewise, the knowledge of natural dye materials was limited. West of the Mississippi, the Indians did not know how to produce a bright red on their porcupine quills, nor could they produce a good green or blue. The same is true for the use of red in textiles in the Southwest. The knowledge of weaving as well as of the materials for weaving cloth, was also limited. In the Southwest, cotton was specially grown and woven into garments. On the Northwest Coast, some use was made of mountain-goat wool and perhaps dog hair. And in the prehistoric Southeast, a small amount of weaving was done with native fibers. The Indians of the Plains utilized a limited quantity of buffalo wool to weave belts, bags, and sashes, but no garments or blankets have been found from this area. However, it is possible that the Plains Indians did at one time make buffalo-hair blankets, since there are a few scattered references to such items in the literature. However, no examples of this work have survived in our museums. Trade cloth and commercial woolen blankets were an early product of the fur trade. They were widely used and eagerly sought by Indians, and soon replaced the native-made product. The eager acceptance of commercial trade goods had the effect of replacing some Indian techniques at a very early date. A kind of resist dye technique used in finger-braided bags and sashes in the Woodland area has never been described in the literature, although it must have been common before 1800.

Because of the Indian's limited knowledge of material and techniques, trade goods, when introduced, had a profound effect on Indian crafts. It is easy to imagine the rapid growth of wood-carving on the Northwest Coast after the introduction of metal knives, but other effects were just as important. Trade cloths gradually replaced leather for garments; glass beads imported from

Venice gradually replaced the use of porcupine and bird quills for decoration; paint pigments such as Chinese vermilion and a good green (verdigris) were eagerly adopted for painted garments as well as for face makeup; and imported dyes such as indigo, madder, and cochineal were used to dye porcupine quills and textiles. In the early years of the trade, pieces of colored cloth were sometimes unraveled to be rewoven into garments, or the cloth was boiled to release the dye for re-dying quills. When aniline dyes were made commonly available, the Indian suddenly had a whole new palette and nearly everything could now be manufactured in a wide variety of bright colors. The same sort of thing occurred with the introduction of commercial oil-base paints on the Northwest Coast. Almost everywhere, the Indians were quick to adapt the bright new materials to their carvings in exchange for their own duller colors. Often a Northwest Coast Indian would take an old mask and have it repainted in the new pigments. When this happened to items such as a house post or a totem pole, the old ritual was still observed; that is, the owner would have to hire someone from another clan to do the painting, and then introduce the newly painted pole with a costly potlatch feast.

Generally, the introduction of trade goods at first caused an elaboration of arts and crafts, and then eventually led to a decline. One example is the use of wooden bowls in the Woodland area. Metal knives naturally made it easier to produce more and better bowls, but later the introduction of metal pots and bowls eliminated the need for handmade wooden ones, and the production declined. A small number of wooden bowls are still being manufactured by Indians who prefer the traditional utensils to the commercially introduced product. In addition, the handmade product is still part of the ceremonial equipment. Older materials and techniques are sometimes retained, despite the variety of new supplies, because conservative religious usage often demands that ritual equipment be manufactured in the time-honored way. Zuni war god figures, even now, are supposedly made from lightning-struck trees, and Hopi Indians still use hand-spun native-grown cotton for the manufacture of prayer sticks.

Some introduced materials had no prototype in older, established media. Items such as glass beads, mirrors, metals, and cloth were brand-new products and special techniques had to be developed to utilize them. Northwest Coast masks suddenly developed eyes made from pieces of mirrors, glass lenses, or even the bottoms of beer bottles. The masks of the Iroquois likewise utilized various metals around the area of the eye. With cloth, came needles and thread, and these new tools and materials were easily adapted. When glass beads were first introduced, the Indians tried to use the same techniques for the new beads that they had been using with porcupine quills. While some of these tech-

19

niques worked with little or no alteration, in others, some modification was necessary. In the case of metals, a wholly unfamiliar material, the Indians had to learn a new technology, since they had no previous experience. Silver ornaments were among the items introduced in trade at an early date. At first, ornaments made in England and later produced by professional silversmiths in the United States and Canada, were given to Indians as gifts to win their allegiance during the time when European powers were vying with one another for a foothold in the New World. Later, silver ornaments were supplied by the traders in return for furs. As soon as the Indians discovered that the ornaments, because of their intrinsic value, could be used as money in the trading posts, they regarded them highly as a decorative and prestige item. When the fur trade declined in importance, the Indians learned from the white man the techniques of working silver, and started to make their own jewelry.

At first the Indians copied the trade forms closely, but in time they developed their own patterns. As the art of working silver moved west from the Iroquois to the Great Lakes, to the Plains, and finally to the Southwest, the forms gradually changed, as each tribe added some kind of innovation to suit its personal tastes. The silverwork of the Navaho Indians today is a flourishing and profitable craft. We often speak of "traditional" Navaho silverwork, yet the tradition started around 1853, and the entire concept is an introduced one. The Navaho, however, are noted not only as borrowers of other people's traditions, but as great innovators. The silver-jewelry concept that the Navaho borrowed from the Indians of the Plains, and from the Spanish in the Southwest, was soon changed into a uniquely Navaho form. The same can be said about other typical Navaho crafts such as blanket-weaving and sand-painting (learned from their Hopi neighbors). The Navaho borrowed the basic idea, and then elaborated it into something distinctly their own.

The techniques used by Indians in producing their arts and crafts were developed over a long period of time by trial and error. These techniques were then passed down from father to son, and from mother to daughter, so that change rarely occurred. Over a period of time, new techniques were developed. If they proved effective they were retained; if not, rejected. This eventually resulted in the simplest and most effective methods of producing everything. Indians tend to be conservative when it comes to change; one reason for this is that frequently the new materials or techniques are just not as good as the old ones. For example, needles and thread have been available to Plains Indians for about 150 years, but they continue to sew beads to their moccasins by using sinew (animal-tendon fiber) and awls. Anyone who has worn a pair of sinew-sewn moccasins will tell you that they last a lot longer than moccasins sewn with thread. The Plains Indians also realized that the new needles and thread worked well for sewing cloth, and so they did not hesitate to use them for this purpose.

Almost everywhere, there was a certain amount of specialization in relation to arts and crafts. We have mentioned the carving specialists of the Northwest Coast and the unique forms of art that are strictly in the domain of the shaman. In contrast, the average Indian family unit is basically self-sufficient and can manufacture all that it needs. Some kinds of specialization develop when there is a limited demand for a certain type of craft. Silverworking seems to fall in this category. While anyone could produce his own jewelry, throughout much of the country, particularly on the Plains and in the Woodland areas, the silversmiths were specialists who usually produced enough silver jewelry for the entire community. Very rarely could they support themselves solely on their silver production, however, so they had to be fairly self-sufficient, just like everyone else in their community.

Many crafts that were once widespread have become limited to production by specialists. Formerly, every woman could make and decorate moccasins, and every man could manufacture wooden bowls and spoons. Now, with the limited demand for these crafts, a group of specialists has appeared to supply both the small Indian demand and that of non-Indians.

Still another factor affecting the role of specialists is the division of labor by sex. Traditionally, men manufacture certain craft products and women, others. On the Plains, there was a sharp distinction between the designs painted on robes by men and those by women. Women painted geometric forms; men, the pictographic war exploits. Plains men made most of the items connected with war and the hunt, while women produced all the household goods and clothing. The items the woman made usually remained hers, so that she owned the lodge and its contents and in the event of a divorce, kept this property.

In the Southwest, men produced the textiles used mainly for ceremonial dress, while women made the pottery and baskets. On the Northwest Coast, men did the carving, boat-building, and bowl-making; the women made the blankets. Almost everywhere, certain crafts were traditionally the province of men and others of women.

In conclusion, we might say that Indians tended to decorate almost everything they used, as time and materials allowed. The motivations for decoration were not unique to American Indians, including as they do the desire for prestige, vanity, pride in craftsmanship, and the giving of gifts to loved ones. The most forceful and original art is usually that related to religion, and this is most commonly vision-inspired. As a general rule, there were no artists as such, but only craftsmen, some of whom were considerably better than others, and their ability was usually recognized. Introductions of new materials and techniques cause an elaboration and then a gradual decline in artistic production. There has been a slow, continual process of acculturation in most Indian groups, and this will lead eventually to complete assimilation, with the resulting disappearance of traditional Indian art forms. The trend seems to be toward the development of new art forms utilizing the age-old Indian heritage, but based on non-Indian techniques and materials.

Footnotes

1. Irvin L. Child, "The Experts and the Bridge of Judgment That Crosses Every Cultural Gap," *Psychology Today,* December 1968, pp. 25–29.

2. J. S. Slotkin, *The Menomini Powwow,* Publications in Anthropology, vol. 4 (1957), Milwaukee Public Museum (for a detailed account of the Sioux woman's vision and the origin of the Dream Dance). For additional data on other vision-induced religions, see J. Mooney, *The Ghost Dance Religion,* Annual Report of the Bureau of American Ethnology (Washington, D.C.: Smithsonian Institution, 1896).

3. R. H. Lowie, *The Religion of the Crow Indians,* Anthropological Papers of the American Museum of Natural History, vol. 25 (1922), pp. 309–444; idem, *The Tobacco Society of the Crow Indians,* Anthropological Papers of the American Museum of Natural History, vol. 21 (1919), pp. 101–200.

4. Dorothy Jean Ray, *Eskimo Masks, Art and Ceremony* (Seattle: University of Washington Press, 1967).

5. William Wildschut, *Crow Indian Medicine Bundles,* edited by John Ewers, Contributions from the Museum of the American Indian, vol. 17 (1960). Clark Wissler, *Ceremonial Bundles of the Blackfoot Indians,* Anthropological Papers of the American Museum of Natural History, vol. 7 (1912), part 2.

6. William N. Fenton, *Masked Medicine Societies of the Iroquois,* Annual Report (Washington, D.C.: Smithsonian Institution, 1940). Robert Ritzenthaler, *Iroquois False-Face Masks,* Milwaukee Public Museum, Publications in Primitive Art, no. 3, 1969.

7. Frank G. Speck, *Oklahoma Delaware Ceremonies, Dances and Feasts,* Memoirs of the American Philosophical Society, vol. 7 (1937); idem, *A Study of the Delaware Big House Ceremony,* Publications of the Pennsylvania Historical Commission, vol. 2 (1931).

8. James H. Howard, "The Kenakuk Religion: An Early 19th Century Revitalization Movement 140 Years Later," *Museum News* (Vermillion: South Dakota Museum, University of South Dakota), vol. 26, nos. 11 and 12.

9. Norman Feder, "American Indian Art Before 1850," *Denver Art Museum Quarterly,* Summer 1965 (for a more complete discussion of why and how early art was collected and preserved).

10. See the various issues of *Beautiful British Columbia* magazine; Winter 1968, pp. 36–38, and Spring 1971, pp. 18–19. The Spring 1971 issue has an article on pp. 30–35 on a newly erected totem pole at Alert Bay in memory of Mungo Martin.

Illustrations

III. (opposite) Frontlet—Tsimshian. 8½" long x 6" wide x 2" deep. Faces and bodies bordered with abalone shells. Painted. Although collected from the Haida, this is in the Tsimshian style. Collection of the National Museum of Man, National Museums of Canada, Ottawa.

IV. Mask—Eskimo. 7½″ high x 5¼″ long x 2″ deep. Wood painted red, white, and black. Collection of the Art Gallery and Museum, Glasgow, Scotland.

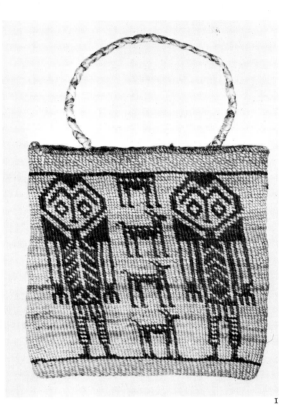

1. Basketry bag—Wasco. 7¾" long x 7½" wide. *Shows the conventionalized human figures typical of this tribe. Collection of the Denver Art Museum.*

2. Shaman's board—Salish (Bay Center, Washington). *6' high x 3' wide. Painted red and black. Shell-inlay eyes. Collection of The American Museum of Natural History, New York.*

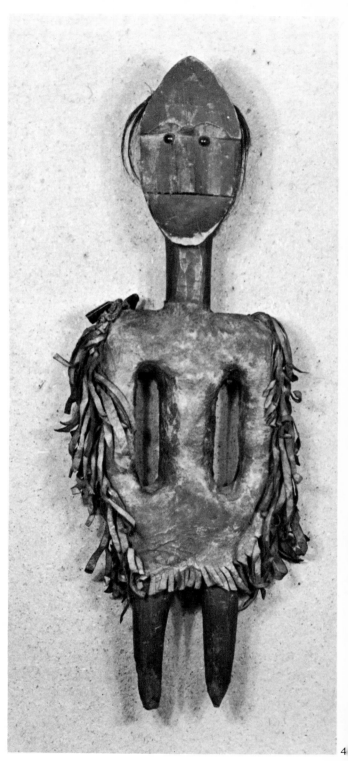

3

4

26

3. Shaman's wand—Quileute (Washington). 15½" long. *Painted red and white. Collection of the Museum of the American Indian, Heye Foundation, New York.*

4. Shaman's wand—Salish. 25¾" long. *Collection of the Denver Art Museum.*

5. Wooden spoon—Wishram-Wasco. 4¼" long x 3⅞" wide x 1⅜" deep; standing figure: 2¾" high. *Collection of the Cranbrook Institute of Science, Bloomfield Hills, Michigan.*

6. Wooden spoon—Wishram. 7¼" long. *Collection of the Royal Scottish Museum, Edinburgh, Scotland.*

5

6

7

8

7. Sheep-horn bowl—Quinault (Washington). 3" high; 7¼" diameter. Collection of the National Museum of Natural History, Smithsonian Institution, Washington, D.C.

8. Carved wooden bowl—Wishram (Spedis, Washington). 11½" deep; top diameter, 15½"; base diameter, 9". Collection of the National Museum of Natural History, Smithsonian Institution, Washington, D.C.

9

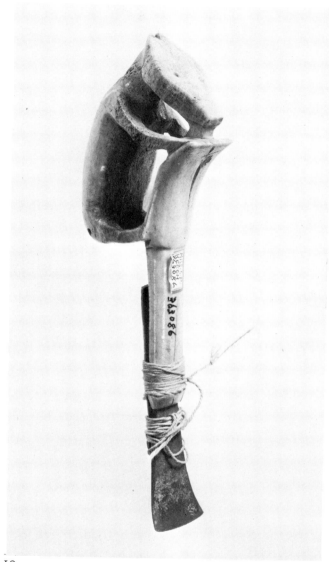

10

9. Antler adze handle—Chinook (?). 8½" long. *Collection of the Peabody Museum, Harvard University, Cambridge, Massachusetts.*

10. Antler adze handle—Wishram-Wasco. 11" *long. Antler handle, metal blade. Collection of the National Museum of Natural History, Smithsonian Institution, Washington, D.C.*

29

11

12

13

11. Spindle whorl—Cowichan. 8¼″ *diameter. Painted brown. Collection of the National Museum of Man, National Museums of Canada, Ottawa.*

12. Wooden spindle whorl—Cowichan. 7½″ *diameter. Collection of the National Museum of Natural History, Smithsonian Institution, Washington, D.C.*

13. Wooden spindle whorl—Cowichan. 7¾″ *diameter. Collection of the National Museum of Natural History, Smithsonian Institution, Washington, D.C.*

14. Figure—Tlingit. 61″ *high. Collection of The American Museum of Natural History, New York.*

15. Carved house post—Nootka (Alberni, B.C.). 12′ 1″ *high. Black, white, and red paint. Collection of the National Museum of Man, National Museums of Canada, Ottawa.*

16. Talking stick (detail)—Kwakiutl. 56″ *long. Such sticks were held by speakers during potlatches. The figure at the top is a man wearing a northern-style clan hat, the center has a row of coppers, and the bottom has a Tsonoqua face. Collection of the Denver Art Museum.*

17. Large carved feast bowl—Kwakiutl (Quatsino). 30″ *long;* 14¾″ *wide at shoulders; circular opening,* 5½″ *deep. Used at winter ceremonies and potlatches. Found in a very old house in a practically deserted village. Collection of the Denver Art Museum.*

18. Face mask—Kwakiutl. 10¼″ *high x* 9¼″ *wide. Represents a Nulmal mask. Collection of the Museum für Völkerkunde, Basel, Switzerland.*

19. "Chief's" mask—Kwakiutl, c. 1870. 12″ *high. Fur brows and whiskers; wood, hair, and paint. Mask is in Tsonoqua form. Collection of Mr. and Mrs. Morton I. Sosland. Photograph by James Enyeart.*

18

20

21

20. Mask—Kwakiutl. 10¼″ *high. Copper, opercula, and hair. Represents a Nulmal mask. Collection of Mr. and Mrs. John H. Hauberg.*

21. Tsonoqua mask—Kwakiutl. 20″ *high. Bearskin and horsehair. Collection of the Milwaukee Public Museum.*

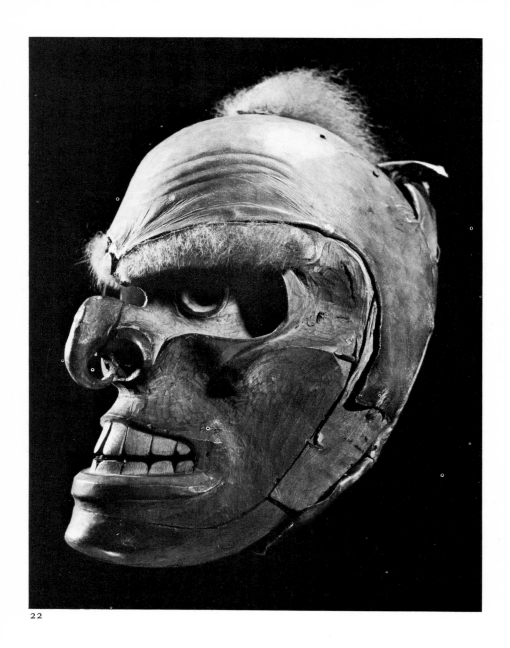

22

22. Wildman-of-the-woods mask (Cockle Hunter)—Kwakiutl. 12½" *high. Bearskin covering scalp, side of head, and chin; bear fur and traces of red paint. Collection of the Milwaukee Public Museum.*

23. Echo mask—Kwakiutl. 11½" *high x* 12⅝" *wide x* 6" *deep. Interchangeable mouths. Collection of the Michael R. Johnson Gallery, Seattle.*

38

23

24

24. Frontlet headdress—Kwakiutl (Kitamaat, B.C.). 7" x 8". *Chief's headdress representing a wolf, attached to a cedar-bark headring. Collection of the Museum of the American Indian, Heye Foundation, New York.*

25. Frontlet headdress—Bella Bella(?). 8¼" high. *Carved and painted wood, with abalone-shell and copper inlay. Collection of Mr. and Mrs. John H. Hauberg.*

26. Mask—Bella Bella (Rivers Inlet). *Represents a Cockle Hunter. Collection of the National Museum of Man, National Museums of Canada, Ottawa.*

25

26

27. Grave monument—Bella Coola. 39¼″ long x 18″ high. *Underside of wings painted black and white; lower beak painted black; traces of white on breast, throat, and eyes. Collection of the National Museum of Man, National Museums of Canada, Ottawa.*

28. Cockle Hunter mask—Bella Coola. 13″ high. *Wood and horsehair. Collection of the Milwaukee Public Museum.*

29. Mask—Tsimshian (Kispiox, Gitksan, Upper Skeena River, B.C.). 7¾″ x 12″. *Represents the face of an old man. Collection of the Museum of the American Indian, Heye Foundation, New York.*

28

29

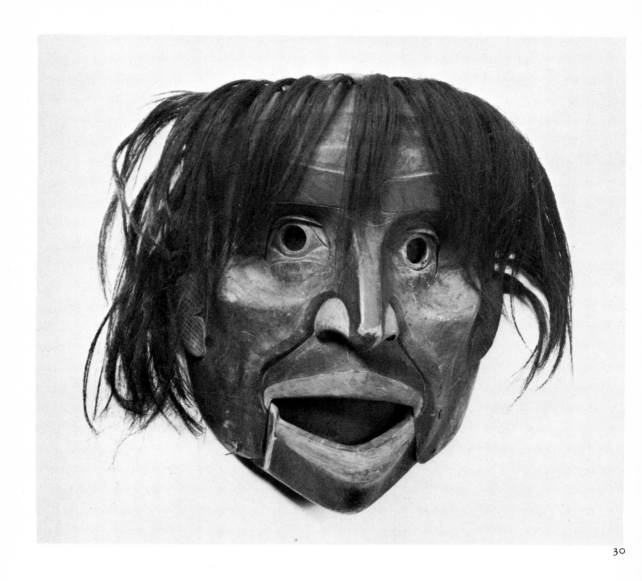

30

30. Mask—Tsimshian (B.C.). 11″ long. Represents a man's face.
Movable eyes and red and black painted decoration. Collection of the
Museum of the American Indian, Heye Foundation, New York.

31. Shaman's charm—Tsimshian (probably of Niska origin but obtained from the Gitksan at Kitwangach, Skeena River, B.C.). *3" high x 4" wide. Ivory inlaid with haliotis shell, carved to represent a sculpin. Collection of the Museum of the American Indian, Heye Foundation, New York.*

32. Ivory charm—Tsimshian. *7½" long. Collection of the National Museum of Natural History, Smithsonian Institution, Washington, D.C.*

32

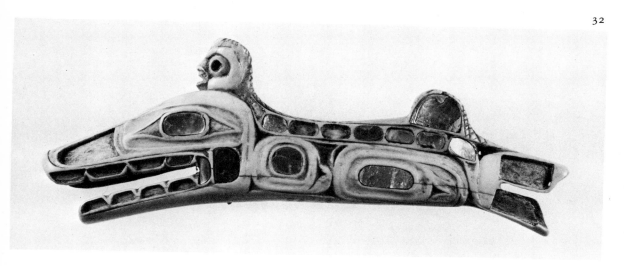

45

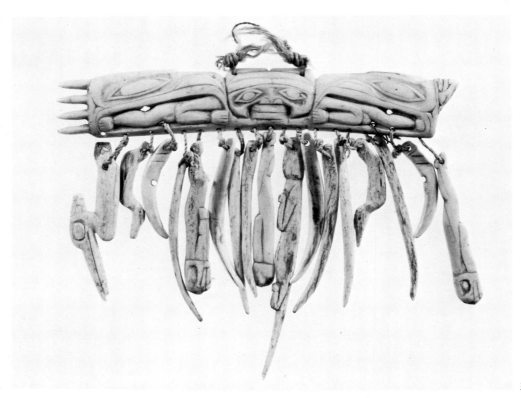

33

34

33. Ivory charm with pendants—Tsimshian (label states, "Haida—Skidegate"). 5½" long x 7" wide. Collection of the National Museum of Natural History, Smithsonian Institution, Washington, D.C.

34. Wooden trunk—Tlingit (Huna, Alaska). 25¼" long x 14¾" wide. Collection of the National Museum of Natural History, Smithsonian Institution, Washington, D.C.

35. Mask—Tlingit. 10¼" high. Collection of the Peabody Museum, Harvard University, Cambridge, Massachusetts.

36

36. Mask—Tlingit, Auk tribe (Pt. Lena, Alaska). 13″ high. *Collection of the Museum of the American Indian, Heye Foundation, New York.*

37. Face mask—Tlingit, Huna tribe (Chicagof Island). 13″ long. *Carved wood representing a spirit of an old woman. A frog spirit emerges from the mouth; on either cheek is a land otter, and on the forehead are land spirits, land otters, and frogs. Russian buttons for eyes, and copper nose and eyebrow decoration. Collection of the Museum of the American Indian, Heye Foundation, New York.*

38. Frontal mask—Tlingit. *Collection of the Museum für Völkerkunde, Basel, Switzerland.*

37

39. Maskette—Tlingit. 4¼″ *high. Represents an eagle spirit. Collection of the Museum of the American Indian, Heye Foundation, New York.*

40. Painted hide armor—Tlingit (Sitka, Alaska). 36″ *long x* 26¾″ *wide. Collection of the Berne Historical Museum, Berne, Switzerland.*

39

40

41

41. Stone mortar—Tlingit(?) (Alaska). 7¼"
high; 12" diameter. Carved from hardstone.
Collection of the National Museum of Natural
History, Smithsonian Institution, Washington,
D.C.

42. Carved puppet head—Haida (Skidegate,
Queen Charlotte Islands, B.C.). 7" long. Col-
lection of the National Museum of Natural
History, Smithsonian Institution, Washington,
D.C.

43. Carved puppet head—Haida (Skidegate,
Queen Charlotte Islands, B.C.). 7⅜" long. Hair
tufts were once inserted all over the top and
hollow back. Collection of the National Museum of Natural History, Smithsonian Institution, Washington, D.C.

42

43

44

44. Opening mask—Haida. 27" *in diameter when open; human face:* 10" *long x* 8" *wide. The outer shell, representing a hawk, can be opened to reveal a human face. Hawk has copper eye pieces, brown hair, and is painted red, black, and white. Human face is painted red and green; hair. Collection of the National Museum of Man, National Museums of Canada, Ottawa.*

45. Wooden whistle with bellows—Haida. *Face portion:* 3½" *long. Collection of the McCord Museum, Montreal, Canada.*

46. Medicine man's rattle—Haida (Clew, Queen Charlotte Islands, B.C.). 12¼" *high. Collection of the Museum of the American Indian, Heye Foundation, New York.*

45

46

47

47. Shaman's dance rattle—Haida (Skidegate, Queen Charlotte Islands, B.C.). 11¾" long; body: 6⅞" long x 5¾" wide. Collection of the National Museum of Natural History, Smithsonian Institution, Washington, D.C.

48. Whistle-rattle—Haida (Skidegate, Queen Charlotte Islands, B.C.). 13¼" long x 8⅞" wide. Collection of the National Museum of Natural History, Smithsonian Institution, Washington, D.C.

49. Small beaver bowl—Haida (Skidegate, Queen Charlotte Islands, B.C.). 8¼" long. Collection of the National Museum of Natural History, Smithsonian Institution, Washington, D.C.

50. Horn bowl—Haida. 6⅛" high x 8¾" wide x 6" deep. Abalone-shell inlay. Collection of the Horniman Museum, London, England.

48

49

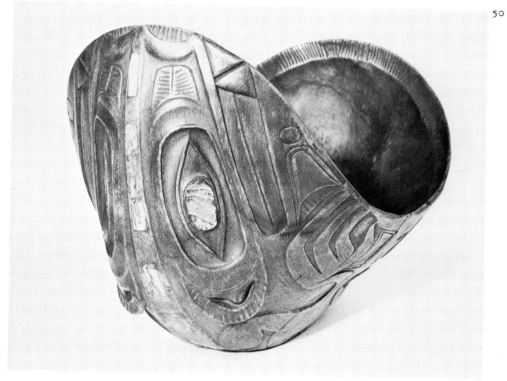

55

51. Horn bowl—Haida. *Collection of the National Musuem of Natural History, Smithsonian Institution, Washington, D.C.*

52. Wooden pipe—Haida. *15¾″ long x 2⅞″ wide. Collection of the Berne Historical Museum, Berne, Switzerland.*

53. Knife—Haida (possibly of Tlingit manufacture). *22½″ long. Copper, with handle representing a human face. Collection of the Museum of the American Indian, Heye Foundation, New York.*

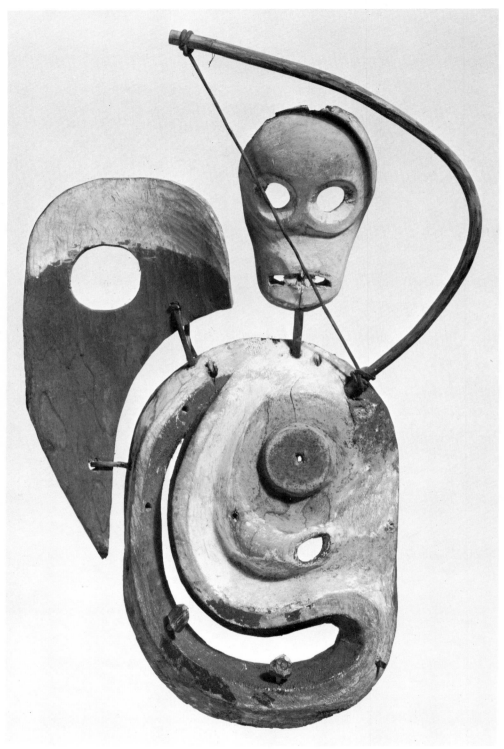

54. Mask—Eskimo (Lower Yukon, Alaska). 16″ high. Wood, pigments, baleen, seal thong. Reddish-brown and white pigmentation. Collection of the Robert H. Lowie Museum of Anthropology, University of California, Berkeley.

55. Mask—Eskimo (Pastolik, Alaska). 14″ high. Wood, pegged-in teeth, feathers, remnants of quills. Red, black, and white pigmentation. Collection of the Robert H. Lowie Museum of Anthropology, University of California, Berkeley.

56. Mask—Eskimo (St. Michael, Norton Sound, Alaska). 15¼″ high. Wood with brown, red, black, and white pigments; bird feathers. Collection of the Robert H. Lowie Museum of Anthropology, University of California, Berkeley.

55

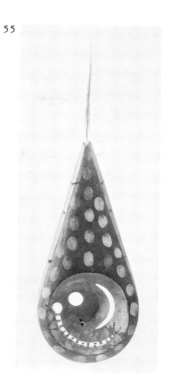

56

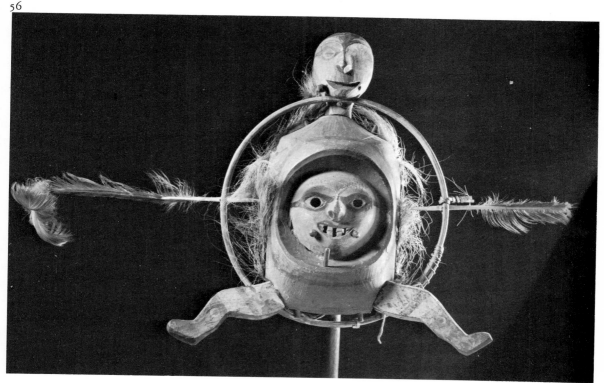

58

57. Mask—Eskimo. 15⅞" long x 11" wide.
Collection of The Brooklyn Museum, Brooklyn, New York.

58. Mask—Eskimo (Goodnews Bay).
Collection of the Milwaukee Public Museum.

59. Mask—Eskimo. *Collection of the Museum für Völkerkunde, Berlin, Germany.*

60. Carved mask—Eskimo (Alaska), c. 1880. 17″ long x 9″ wide. *Wood. Labret in right corner of mouth and hole for another in left corner. A single rod runs part way around the edge of the mask. Collection of the Denver Art Museum.*

60

61

62

61. Mask—Eskimo (St. Michael, Norton Sound, Alaska). 13½" long x 16¾" wide, less feathers. White face with red trim; seventeen feathers. Mouth has wooden and enameled teeth. Animal paw is attached to shield. Collection of the National Museum of Natural History, Smithsonian Institution, Washington, D.C.

62. Mask—Eskimo (Askeenick, near Cape Romanzoff, Alaska). 9½" high. Small mask. Grinning mouth with diamond-shaped teeth. Four eyes, two on either side, ringed with black. Red and black trim. Worn at Feasts for the Dead. Collection of the National Museum of Natural History, Smithsonian Institution, Washington, D.C.

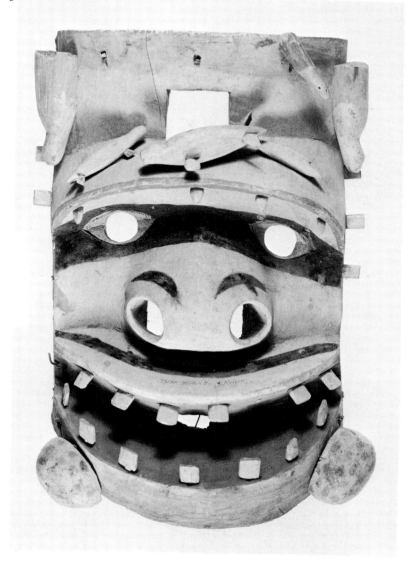

63. Mask—Eskimo (Norton Sound, Alaska). 22″ *high. Collection of the National Museum of Natural History, Smithsonian Institution, Washington, D.C.*

64

64. Visor—Eskimo. *Collection of the Museum für Völkerkunde, Berlin, Germany.*

65. Finger masks—Eskimo. *Collection of the Museum für Völkerkunde, Berlin, Germany.*

65

66

67

66. Finger masks—Eskimo (left to right: Stebbins Island, off St. Michael, Norton Sound, Alaska; St. Michael, Norton Sound, Alaska; Rasbonsky, Alaska). *Mask at left, with skin and hair inserted in marginal groove: 5" long; 3¼" diameter. Collection of the National Museum of Natural History, Smithsonian Institution, Washington, D.C.*

67. Doll—Eskimo (Diomede Island, Alaska). *8" high. Carved wood with inlaid ivory eyes; decorated with ivory earrings and beaded nose ornament. Collection of the Museum of the American Indian, Heye Foundation, New York.*

68. Wooden figure—Eskimo (Kuskokwim River, Alaska). 19″ *high. Collection of the National Museum of Natural History, Smithsonian Institution, Washington, D.C.*

69. Dance stick—Hunkpapa Sioux (Standing Rock Reservation, North Dakota). 34½" long. *Collection of the Museum of the American Indian, Heye Foundation, New York.*

70. Horse dance stick—Hunkpapa Sioux (Standing Rock Reservation, North Dakota). 32" long. *Collection of the Museum of the American Indian, Heye Foundation, New York.*

69

70

71

72

73

71. Tomahawk Society wand—Arapaho. *37" long. Carried by members of the lowest degree in the Tomahawk Lodge, also known as "The First Dance." Head carving is said to represent a buffalo. Collection of Mr. James Economos.*

72. Human effigy wand (detail)—Assinaboin or Sioux (Ft. Peck). *33" long x 3⅛" wide. Red paint, fire coloration. Use unknown. Collection of the Chandler-Pohrt Collection, Great Lakes Indian Museum, Cross Village, Michigan.*

73. Pipe bowl—Sioux(?) (Pipestone, Minnesota). *8" long x 4" wide x 2" deep. Carved dragonhead of pipestone. Collection of the Minnesota Historical Society, St. Paul.*

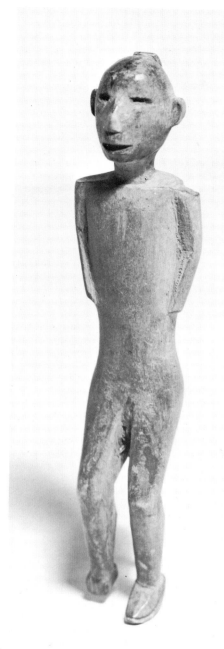

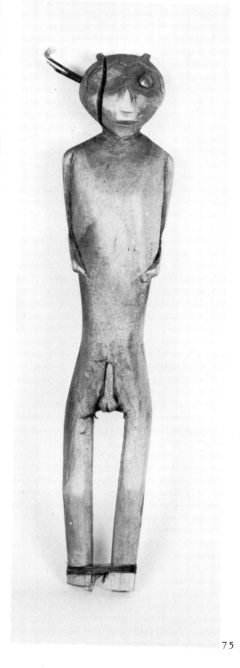

74

75

74. Tree-dweller doll—Santee Sioux. *6″ high x 1½″ wide x ¾″ thick. Collection of the Minnesota Historical Society, St. Paul.*

75. Tree-dweller doll—Santee Sioux. *6½″ high. Used in the Sioux version of the Grand Medicine Lodge. Collection of the State Historical Society of Colorado, Denver.*

76

76. Mirror board—Omaha. 14″ *high x 6⅜″* *wide. Iron upholstery tacks and brass pins. Collection of the Chandler-Pohrt Collection, Great Lakes Indian Museum, Cross Village, Michigan.*

77. Food bowl—Sisseton Sioux (North Dakota). 16″ *maximum diameter. Wood, with carved bird's head on rim. Used in the Medicine Dance. Collection of the Museum of the American Indian, Heye Foundation, New York.*

77

78

79

78. Wooden bowl in beaver form—tribe unknown (Great Lakes). 25½″ *long x* 13″ *wide x* 4″ *high. Collection of The Detroit Institute of Arts.*

79. Wooden effigy bowl—Winnebago. 6¾″ *diameter; human head carved on rim:* 1½″ *high x* 3″ *deep. Collection of the Denver Art Museum.*

80. Cow-horn spoons—Sioux. 9¼″ high x 4¾″ wide. Handles wrapped with dyed quills; carved bird's head on the end of handles. Collection of the National Museum of Natural History, Smithsonian Institution, Washington, D.C.

81. Cow-horn spoon—Sioux. 10¼″ long. Collection of the Chandler-Pohrt Collection, Great Lakes Indian Museum, Cross Village, Michigan.

82. War club—Iowa (Oklahoma). 21¾″ long.
From a buffalo war bundle. Collection of the
Museum of the American Indian, Heye Foun-
dation, New York.

82

83. Catlinite head of a war club—Sioux, 1900.
Club: 24¾″ long; head: 4⅛″ long. Face on one
end of head. Collection of Mr. L. D. Bax.

83

75

84. Stone-headed war club (detail) — Sioux. 19½" x 7¼". *Buffalo head carved from a soft, banded, gray stone. Bead-wrapped handle. Collection of the Denver Art Museum.*

85. War club—possibly Iroquois. *Inlaid with pieces of shell and wampum beads. Collection of the Danish National Museum, Copenhagen.*

85

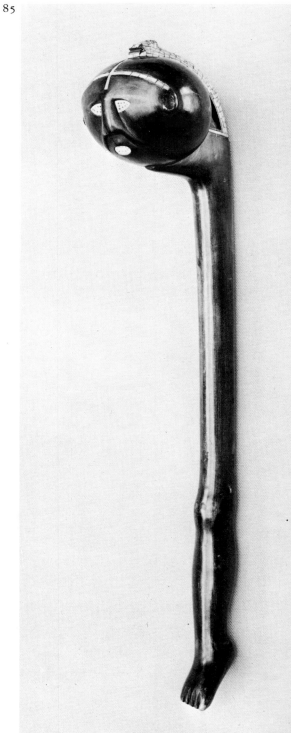

84

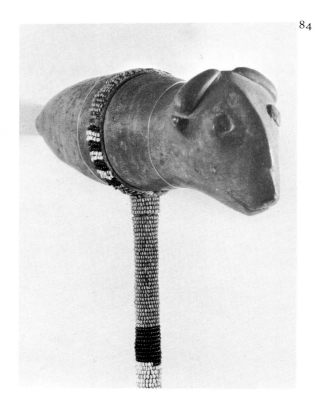

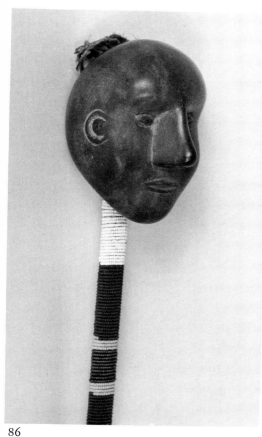

86

86. Stone-headed war club (detail)—Sioux (Rosebud, South Dakota). 24″ long x 4⅝″ high x 4″ deep. Head represents a man's face. Red, white, blue, and yellow seed beads on handle; remnants of feathers on head. Said to have belonged to Rain-in-the-Face. Collection of the Chandler-Pohrt Collection, Great Lakes Indian Museum, Cross Village, Michigan.

87. Rawhide rattle—Blackfoot (?), possibly Cheyenne (?). 10″ high. Eagle claws form horns. Painted design depicts a spirit. Horsehair scalplock. Collection of the Museum of the American Indian, Heye Foundation, New York.

87

88

88. Pipe and carved stem—Sioux, 1880–1900. *Stem: 24" long; bowl: 8¾" long x 4⅝" high. Collection of Mr. L. D. Bax.*

89. Catlinite pipe bowl—probably Santee Sioux. *5⅞" long x 3⅞" high. Seated human figure; ears pierced with wire earrings; wire wound around the neck. Collection of the Cranbrook Institute of Science, Bloomfield Hills, Michigan.*

89

90. Catlinite pipe bowl—Sioux(?). 7" long x 3¼" high. Seated human figure with tomahawk in right hand. Collection of the Chandler-Pohrt Collection, Great Lakes Indian Museum, Cross Village, Michigan.

91. Catlinite pipe bowl—possibly Sioux. 9½" long. Represents horse and rider. Collection of Royal Scottish Museum, Edinburgh, Scotland.

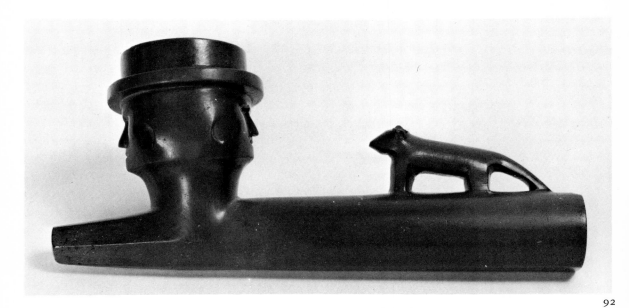

92

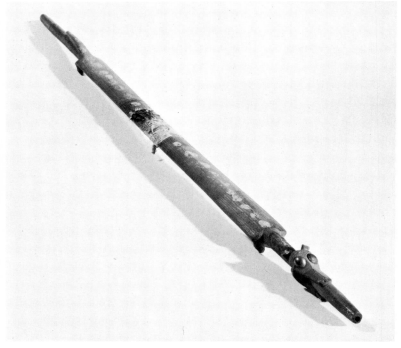

93

92. Catlinite pipe bowl—Iowa(?). 8½″ long x 3⅝″ high. *Janus-faced. Collection of the Chandler-Pohrt Collection, Great Lakes Indian Museum, Cross Village, Michigan.*

93. Wood pipestem—Sioux (made at Ft. Snelling, 1833–36). 26″ long. *Collection of The Brooklyn Museum.*

94

95

94. Shield—probably Arapaho (called Mandan by the Heye Foundation). *19″ diameter. Buffalo hide with painted deerskin cover. Black and green painted decoration with design of a snapping turtle. Pendant eagle feathers and trade bells. Collection of the Museum of the American Indian, Heye Foundation, New York.*

95. Wooden pipe bowl with stem—tribe unknown. *Eyes inlaid with pieces of black coral. Collection of the Danish National Museum, Copenhagen.*

96. Painted shield—Sioux. 20″ x 22″ x 4″. Painted rawhide decorated with feathers and bells. Collection of the Minnesota Historical Society, St. Paul.

97. Pictographic painting—Sioux. 2′ 11″ high x 7′ 3″ wide. The painting on muslin depicts the war exploits of a single man. Collection of the Denver Art Museum.

98

98. Painted Ghost Dance shirt—Arapaho. *Blue background; painted red, green, dark blue, brown. Magpie feathers hang from bib. Collection of the Chandler-Pohrt Collection, Great Lakes Indian Museum, Cross Village, Michigan.*

99. Painted skin shirt—called Sauk but probably Santee Sioux. *3' 11" high x 4' 8" wide. Collection of the Berne Historical Museum, Berne, Switzerland.*

99

English – Performing the dreams of Black Tail Deer
Dakota – Sírite Sakda Kaga.

84

100. Pictographic drawing on paper—Sioux (Rosebud, South Dakota), c. 1890. 5¾" high x 9" wide. Pencil and colored pencil on paper. Title: "Dreams about Blacktail Deer and how he performed the same." Collection of the Chandler-Pohrt Collection, Great Lakes Indian Museum, Cross Village, Michigan.

101. Pictographic drawing on paper—Sioux (Rosebud, South Dakota), c. 1890. 5¾" high x 8⅛" wide. Ink and colored pencil. Title: "Performing the dreams of Blacktail Deer." Collection of the Chandler-Pohrt Collection, Great Lakes Indian Museum, Cross Village, Michigan.

102. Kachina mask—Zuni. 9¾" high x 26" wide. Represents Sayatasha, Rain Priest of the North. Leather decorated with hair and feathers, cotton, wood, and fur. Collection of The Brooklyn Museum.

103. Buffalo fetish stone—Zuni. 3¾" high x 6" wide x 2½" deep. Collection of the Denver Art Museum.

104. Stone bird fetish—Zuni. 5½″ high x 2½″ wide. Basalt with turquoise eyes, collar, and breast. Collection of the Taylor Museum, Colorado Springs Fine Arts Center.

105. Altar carving—Zuni. 10¾″ high x 11¼″ wide. Carved wood buffalo head used on altar of Buffalo Clan during Shalako dances. Cottonwood painted black, white, yellow, and red; black horsehair. Collection of the Taylor Museum, Colorado Springs Fine Arts Center.

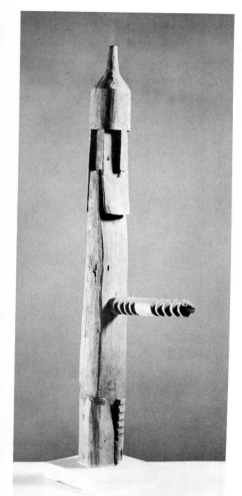

106. War god—Zuni. 30⅝" high. *Collection of The Brooklyn Museum.*

107. Kachina doll—Zuni, Salimopia-Anahoho. 14⅝" high. *Wood painted white. Collection of The Brooklyn Museum.*

108. Kachina doll—Zuni. 10″ *high x* 4¾″ *wide. Wood. Collection of The Brooklyn Museum.*

109. Kachina doll—Zuni. 21″ *high x* 7¾″ *wide. Wood. Collection of The Brooklyn Museum.*

110. Kachina doll—Hopi, Sio Calako. 16⅞″ *high. Collection of the Peabody Museum, Harvard University, Cambridge, Massachusetts.*

V. Shield—Sioux. 17¾" diameter. Painted on leather, with feathers. Collection of the Denver Art Museum.

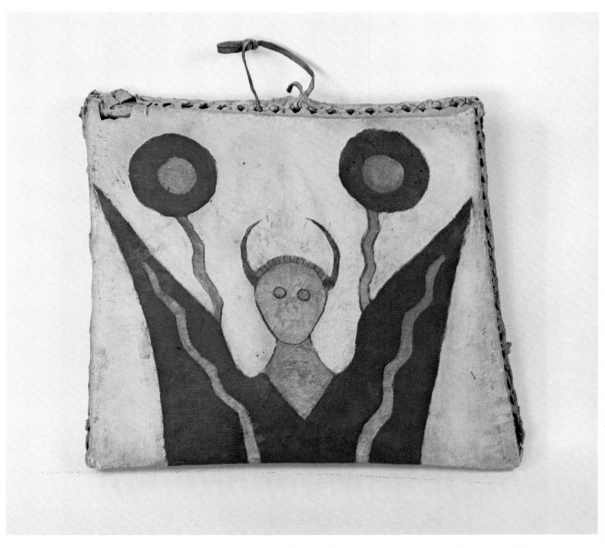

VI. Painted skin drum—Assinaboin or Sioux (Ft. Peck), c. 1885. 17½″ x 16″. *White and black repainted. Skin laced on wood frame. Collection of the Chandler-Pohrt Collection, Great Lakes Indian Museum, Cross Village, Michigan.*

111. Kachina doll—Hopi. 18″ *high. Collection of the Peabody Museum, Harvard University, Cambridge, Massachusetts.*

112

112. Double altar Kachina dolls—Hopi. 10″
high x 12″ wide. Collection of The American
Museum of Natural History, New York.

113. Carving of a human figure—Hopi,
c. 1870. 21″ high. Wood with separate arms.
Anonymous collector.

114. Painted leather pouch and wooden doll—Apache. *Pouch: bag, 3½" long x 9½" wide; cord, 3' long. Doll: 4¾" long x 1½" wide x ¼" thick. Doll has a double choker of white pony beads around neck; trimmed with two white commercial buttons and one long white feather; eyes are glass beads. Pouch contains doll. Collection of the Denver Art Museum.*

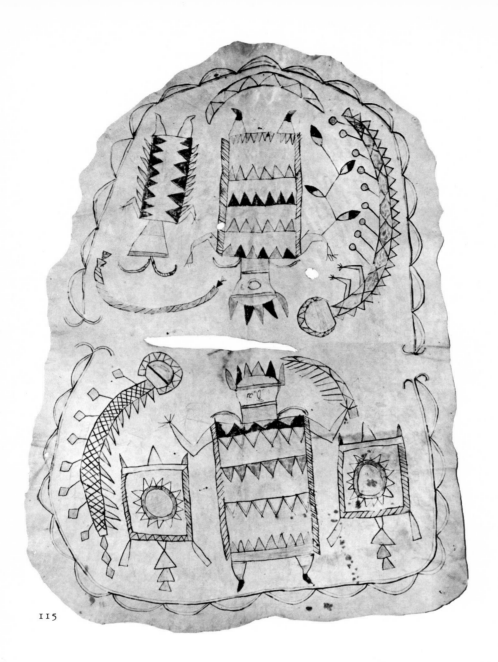

115

115. Painted cape—Chiricahua Apache. 47″ *long. Painted skin used as medicine shirt. Collection of the Museum of the American Indian, Heye Foundation, New York.*

116. Clay figure—Cocopa (Lower California). 10″ *high. Collection of the Peabody Museum, Harvard University, Cambridge, Massachusetts.*

117. Clay doll—Mohave. 9¾″ *high. Collection of the Peabody Museum, Harvard University, Cambridge, Massachusetts.*

116

117

93

118

118. Doll—Mohave. 8¼″ *high. Brown pottery with yarn and beads. Collection of The Brooklyn Museum.*

119. Doll with child—Mohave. 9″ *high. Collection of the National Museum of Natural History, Smithsonian Institution, Washington, D.C.*

94

95

120. Wood effigy—Klamath (Oregon), 21¾″ high. *Collection of the Peabody Museum, Harvard University, Cambridge, Massachusetts.*

121. Painted drum—Arapaho, 1890. 14¾″ diameter. *Collection of Mr. L. D. Bax.*

122. Wooden pipe bowl (detail)—Ojibwa (White Earth Reservation, Minnesota). 5″ x 2½″ x 3″ *Bowl in the shape of a human head. Collection of the Minnesota Historical Society, St. Paul.*

121

122

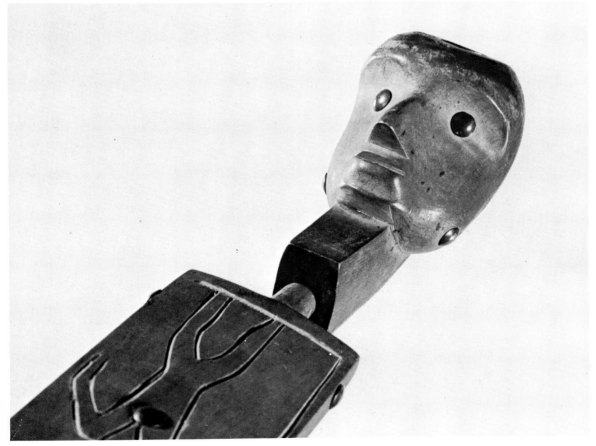

123

124

123. Stone pipe bowl—Ojibwa(?). 2¾″ *high x* 7⅜″ *long. Collection of the Royal Ontario Museum, Toronto, Canada.*

124. Wooden pipe bowl with metal inlay— *tribe unknown.* 7″ *long x* 3½″ *high. Bird feathers for sideburns, brass wire over ears. Collection of the McCord Museum, Montreal, Canada.*

125

126

125. Pipe bowl of soapstone—tribe unknown (Great Lakes?). 5¾″ long. *Human face and bird. Collection of the Museum für Völkerkunde, Basel, Switzerland.*

126. Carved wooden head—Cree (Old Yellow Mill Trail, Manitoba). 4⅝″ high. *Collection of the Royal Ontario Museum, Toronto, Canada.*

 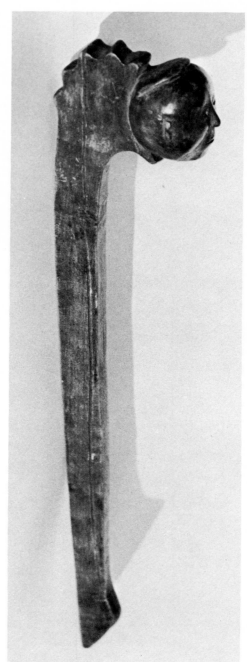

127. Antler carving—Cree. 7″ long. *Quirt handle (?). Collection of the Royal Ontario Museum, Toronto, Canada.*

128. Small ball-headed war club—Winnebago (Black River Falls, Wisconsin). 15″ long. *Face on ball. Traces of red paint. Collection of Mr. Loren D. Herrington.*

129. Wooden bowl in beaver form—Kaskaskia(?). *Collection of The University Museum, University of Pennsylvania, Philadelphia.*

130. Small wooden bowl from Medicine Lodge—Winnebago (Sioux City, Iowa). *3¼" long x 2¾" wide x ¼" deep. Bird effigy; two brass tacks form the eyes. Collection of the Cranbrook Institute of Science, Bloomfield Hills, Michigan.*

131. Mide doll—tribe unknown. *Carved wood. Collection of Mr. George Terasaki.*

132. Juggler dolls—Menominee. *9″ high x 2¼″ wide. Collection of the Milwaukee Public Museum.*

133. Mide doll—Ojibwa. 17″ *high. Collection of the Milwaukee Public Museum.*

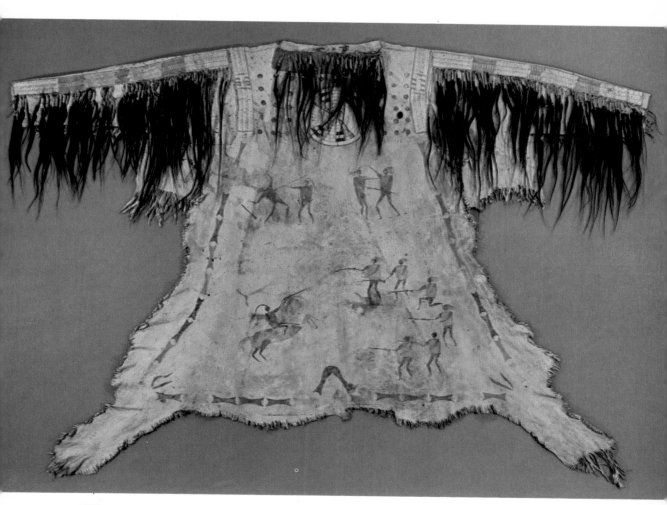

VII. Painted skin shirt—Yanktonai Sioux. *Belonged to Wanata, a well-known chief. Collection of the Royal Scottish Museum, Edinburgh, Scotland.*

VIII. Model cradle—Mohave. *Fiber and wood cradle:* 17¾″ *long x* 4¾″ *wide; clay doll:* 11¼″ *long. Collection of the Denver Art Museum.*

134. Carved wooden doll—Ojibwa. 11¼″ *high. Head was carved separately and inserted so that it can be made to move back and forth. Used in Mide magic. Two brass tacks for eyes. Left half of face painted red with Chinese vermilion; red also on shoulders; no other traces of paint left. Collection of the Denver Art Museum.*

135. Mide doll—Ojibwa (Berens River Band of Salteaux, Lake Winnipeg, Canada). *14″ high. Wooden image from medicine bundle. Used as "bad medicine" to wish evil on a person. Collection of the Museum of the American Indian, Heye Foundation, New York.*

136. Stick rattle—Ojibwa. *10″ long. Bird form. Collection of Mr. James Economos.*

137. Love doll (male)—Prairie Potawatomi (Crandon, Wisconsin). *9" high x 2" wide. Two small nails serve as the eyes; ears are pierced. Wood has traces of red rubbed into grain. Red wool leggings. Collection of the Cranbrook Institute of Science, Bloomfield Hills, Michigan.*

138. Mirror board (detail)—probably Woodland. *25" long x 3¾" wide at top. Pair of horse heads at top. Collection of the Chandler-Pohrt Collection, Great Lakes Indian Museum, Cross Village, Michigan.*

138

139. Carved wooden heddle-frame—Fox (Tama, Iowa). 13¼″ x 9″. *Made by John Young Bear. Used for weaving beaded bands. Collection of the Chandler-Pohrt Collection, Great Lakes Indian Museum, Cross Village, Michigan.*

140. Crooked knife—Ojibwa (Beaver Island, Michigan). *Handle: 6¼″ long; blade: 4¼″ long. Wrapped in string and leather covered. Collection of the Chandler-Pohrt Collection, Great Lakes Indian Museum, Cross Village, Michigan.*

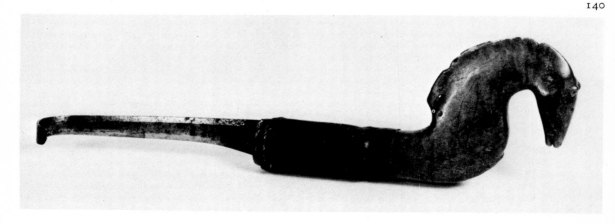

141. False Face mask—Seneca (Cattaraugus Reservation, New York) or possibly Tonawanda. 9¾″ long x 6¼″ wide. Unpainted. *Thick eyebrows and lower lip are colored with charcoal. This smiling mask is a beggar- or dancing-mask of the type worn by small boys when they go around to houses begging for tobacco at the Mid-winter Festival. Collection of the Cranbrook Institute of Science, Bloomfield Hills, Michigan.*

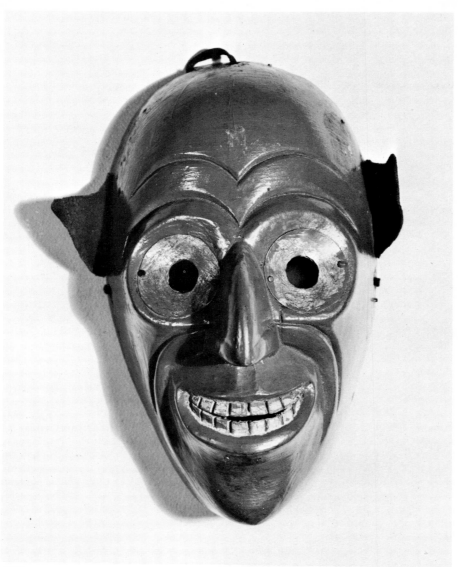

142

142. False Face mask—Seneca (western New York). 10″ long. Orange paint. Tin eye plates; hide ears. Collection of the Milwaukee Public Museum.

143. Mask—Seneca (Cattaraugus Reservation, New York). 11″ long. Collection of the Museum of the American Indian, Heye Foundation, New York.

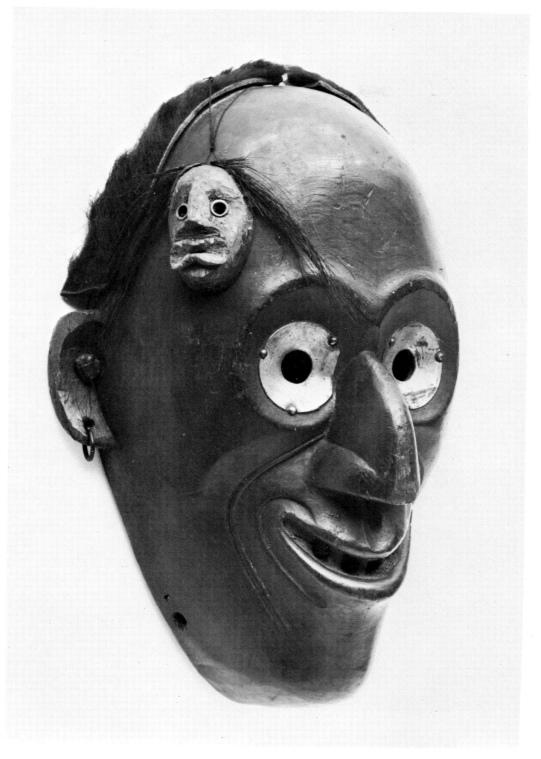

143

144

145

144. False Face mask—Iroquois (Grand River Reservation). *Painted red with yellow teeth; black brow ridges and lips. Black horsehair; brass eyeplates. Collection of the Milwaukee Public Museum.*

145. False Face mask—Iroquois (New York). 10¼" long. *Traces of black paint. White braided horsehair; brass eyeplates. Collection of the Milwaukee Public Museum.*

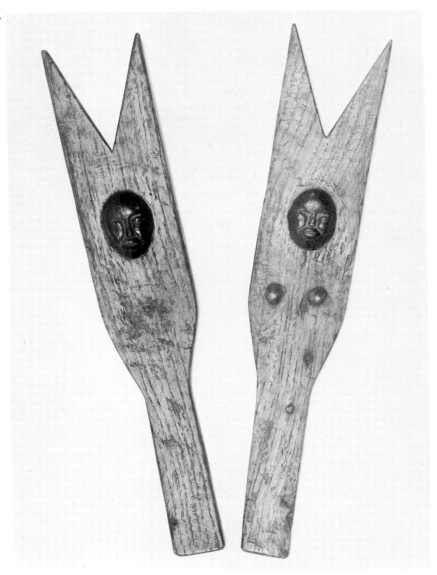

146. False Face mask—Iroquois (Six Nations Reservation, Grand River, Ontario). 10½″ long x 7″ wide x 6″ deep. *Painted black with red lips and traces of red on orbital ridges. Horsehair on head. Collection of the National Museum of Natural History, Smithsonian Institution, Washington, D.C.*

147. Drumsticks—Delaware (Oklahoma). 19″ long. Blade: 3½″ wide; face: 2½″ long x 1¾″ wide. *Carved oak wood. Used on the ninth to twelfth nights of the Big House ceremony. Collection of the Denver Art Museum.*

148. Carved house post—Delaware (Big House near Copan, Oklahoma). 15¼″ high x 9″ wide. *Painted half red and half black. Collection of the Woolaroc Museum, Bartlesville, Oklahoma.*

149. Carved house post with face on each side —Delaware (Copan, Oklahoma). *46″ high. Base block: 11½″ wide x 13½″ long; face shown: 20⅜″ high x 11¼″ wide. Collection of the Philbrook Art Center, Tulsa.*

150. Carved wooden figure—Caddo. 6¾″ *high. Hard wood. Traces of paint. Human hair wig and mustachio. Holds sacred bundle between knees in doeskin bag. Collection of the National Museum of Natural History, Smithsonian Institution, Washington, D.C.*

Bibliography

The first two references are bibliographies that will help in locating additional data on many subjects.

MURDOCK, GEORGE PETER. *Ethnographic Bibliography of North America.* 3d ed. New Haven, Conn.: Human Relations Area Files, 1960. (A listing of references by tribe and area.)

HARDING, ANNE D., and BOLLING, PATRICIA. "Bibliography of North American Indian Art." Mimeographed. Washington, D.C., 1939. (Out of print. References listed by technique; a handy guide but outdated.)

ADAIR, JOHN. *The Navaho and Pueblo Silversmiths.* Norman: University of Oklahoma Press, 1944.

AMSDEN, CHARLES. *Navaho Weaving.* Santa Ana, Calif.: Fine Arts Press, 1934.

APPLETON, L. H. *Indian Art of the Americas.* New York: Charles Scribner's Sons, 1950.

BARBEAU, MARIUS. *Totem Poles.* 2 vols. Bulletin No. 119, Anthropological Series No. 30. Ottawa: National Museum of Canada, 1930.

———. *Haida Carvers in Argillite.* Bulletin No. 139. Ottawa: National Museum of Canada, 1957.

———. *Indian Days on the Western Prairies.* Bulletin No. 163. Ottawa: National Museum of Canada, 1960. (Good illustrations of pictographic painting, but text is a collection of myths.)

BIRKET-SMITH, KEJ. *The Eskimos.* New York: E. P. Dutton, 1936.

BOURKE, J. G. *Medicine Men of the Apache.* 9th Annual Report of the Bureau of American Ethnology. Washington, D.C.: Smithsonian Institution, 1892.

BRODY, J. J. *Indian Painters and White Patrons.* Albuquerque: University of New Mexico Press, 1971.

BUSHNELL, DAVID I., JR. *Drawings by George Gibbs in the Far Northwest, 1849–1851.*

Smithsonian Miscellaneous Collections, vol. 97, no. 8. Washington, D.C.: Smithsonian Institution, 1938.

COLTON, H. S. *Hopi Kachina Dolls.* Albuquerque: University of New Mexico Press, 1959.

COVARRUBIAS, MIGUEL. *The Eagle, the Jaguar, and the Serpent.* New York: Alfred A. Knopf, 1954.

DAVIS, ROBERT TYLER. *Native Arts of the Pacific Northwest.* Palo Alto, Calif.: Stanford University Press, 1949.

DOCKSTADER, FREDERICK J. *Indian Art in America.* Greenwich, Conn.: New York Graphic Society, 1961.

———. *The Kachina and the White Man.* Bulletin No. 35. Bloomfield Hills, Mich.: Cranbrook Institute of Science, 1954.

DOUGLAS, FREDERIC H., and D'HARNONCOURT, RENÉ. *Indian Art of the United States.* New York: Museum of Modern Art, 1941.

DRUCKER, PHILIP. *Indians of the Northwest Coast.* New York: AMS Press, 1963. (An excellent and complete discussion of the people and the art.)

DUFF, WILSON; HOLM, BILL; and REID, BILL. *Arts of the Raven—Masterworks by the Northwest Coast Indian.* Vancouver, B.C.: Vancouver Art Gallery, 1967.

DUNN, DOROTHY. *American Indian Paintings of the Southwest and Plains Area.* Albuquerque: University of New Mexico Press, 1971.

———. "The Development of Modern American Indian Painting." *El Palacio* (Santa Fe), vol. 58, no. 11, pp. 331–53.

EWERS, JOHN C. *Blackfeet Crafts.* Lawrence, Kans.: Haskell Institute, 1945.

———. *Plains Indian Painting.* Palo Alto, Calif.: Stanford University Press, 1939.

EWERS, JOHN C., and WILDSCHUT, WILLIAM. *Crow Indian Medicine Bundles.* Contributions of the Museum of the American Indian, vol. 17. New York: Museum of the American Indian, 1960.

FEDER, NORMAN. *American Indian Art.* New York: Harry Abrams, 1971.

———. *Art of the Eastern Plains Indians.* New York: Brooklyn Museum, 1964.

———. *North American Indian Painting.* New York: Museum of Primitive Art, 1967.

FEDER, NORMAN, and MALIN, EDWARD. *Indian Art of the Northwest Coast.* Denver: Denver Art Museum, 1962.

FENTON, WILLIAM N. *Masked Medicine Societies of the Iroquois.* Annual Report. Washington, D.C.: Smithsonian Institution, 1940.

GODDARD, P. E. *Indians of the Southwest.* New York: American Museum of Natural History, 1931.

GLUBOK, SHIRLEY. *The Art of the North American Indian.* New York: Harper & Row, 1964. (A good book for children.)

GUNTHER, ERNA. *Art in the Life of the Northwest Coast Indians.* Catalogue of the Rasmussen Collection at the Portland Art Museum. Seattle, 1966.

———. *Northwest Coast Indian Art.* Catalogue of the Seattle World's Fair. Seattle, 1962.

GUNTHER, ERNA, and HAEBERLIN, HERMAN. *The Indians of Puget Sound.* Publications in Anthropology, vol. 4. Seattle: University of Washington Press, 1930.

HARNER, MICHAEL J., and ELSASSER, ALBERT B. *Art of the Northwest Coast.* Catalogue of an exhibition at the Robert H. Lowie Museum of Anthropology. Berkeley, Calif., 1965.

HASSRICK, ROYAL B. *Indian Art of the Americas.* Denver: Denver Art Museum, 1960.

HAWTHORN, AUDREY. *Art of the Kwakiutl Indians.* Seattle: University of Washington Press, 1967. (A well-illustrated catalogue of the collections of the University of British Columbia Museum.)

HOFFMAN, W. J. *The Graphic Art of the Eskimo.* Annual Report of the Bureau of American Ethnology. Washington, D.C.: Smithsonian Institution, 1895.

———. *The Medewiwin or 'Grand Medicine Society' of the Ojibwa.* Annual Report of the Bureau of American Ethnology. Washington, D.C.: Smithsonian Institution, 1886.

HOLM, BILL. *Northwest Coast Indian Art.* Seattle: University of Washington Press, 1965. (Detailed analysis of two-dimensional art.)

HOWARD, JAMES. "Pan-Indian Culture of Oklahoma." *The Scientific Monthly,* November 1955, pp. 215–20.

INVERARITY, ROBERT BRUCE. *Art of the Northwest Coast Indians.* Berkeley: University of California Press, 1950.

JENNES, DIAMOND. *The Indians of Canada.* Bulletin No. 65. Ottawa: National Museum of Canada, 1932.

KRICKEBERG, WALTER. *Ältere Ethnographica aus Nordamerika im Berliner Museum für Völkerkunde.* Berlin: Baessler Archiv, Neue Folge, Band II, 1954. (Good discussion of early material in German museums.)

LaBARRE, WESTON. *The Peyote Cult.* Publications in Anthropology. New Haven: Yale University Press, 1938.

LOWIE, ROBERT H. *Indians of the Plains.* New York: McGraw-Hill, 1954.

———. *Crow Indian Art.* Anthropological Papers, vol. 21, part 4. New York: American Museum of Natural History, 1922.

LYFORD, CARRIE A. *Iroquois Crafts.* Lawrence, Kans.: Haskell Institute, 1945.

———. *Ojibwa Crafts.* Lawrence, Kans.: Haskell Institute, 1945.

———. *Quill and Beadwork of the Western Sioux.* Lawrence, Kans.: Haskell Institute, 1940.

MALLERY, GARRICK. *Picture Writing of American Indians.* Annual Report of the Bureau of American Ethnology. Washington, D.C.: Smithsonian Institution, 1893.

MILLS, GEORGE. *Navaho Art and Culture.* Colorado Springs: Taylor Museum, Colorado Springs Fine Arts Center, 1959. (An excellent treatment of the role of art in Navaho life.)

MOCHON, MARION JOHNSON. *Masks of the Northwest Coast.* Publications in Primitive Art, no. 2. Milwaukee: Milwaukee Public Museum, 1966.

MOONEY, J. *The Ghost Dance Religion.* Annual Report of the Bureau of American Ethnology. Washington, D.C.: Smithsonian Institution, 1896.

MORGAN, L. H. *The League of the Iroquois.* Edited by H. M. Lloyd. 2 vols. in one. New York: Dodd, Mead & Co., 1922.

MUSÉE DE L'HOMME. *Masterpieces of Indian and Eskimo Art from Canada*. Paris: Société des Amis du Musée de l'Homme, 1969. (Text in both French and English.)

PRINCETON UNIVERSITY ART MUSEUM. *Art of the Northwest Coast*. Princeton, N.J., 1969.

RAY, DOROTHY JEAN. *Eskimo Masks, Art and Ceremony*. Seattle: University of Washington Press, 1967.

RITZENTHALER, ROBERT. *Iroquois False-Face Masks*. Publications in Primitive Art, no. 3. Milwaukee: Milwaukee Public Museum, 1969.

SIEBERT, ERNA, and FORMAN, WERNER. *North American Indian Art*. London: Paul Hamlyn, Ltd., 1967. (A catalogue of Northwest Coast art in Russian museums.)

SKINNER, ALANSON. *Material Culture of the Menomini*. Indian Notes and Monographs, vol. 20. New York: Museum of the American Indian, 1921.

SLOAN, JOHN, and LA FARGE, OLIVER. *Introduction to American Indian Art*. Catalogue for exposition of Indian tribal arts, New York, 1931.

SLOTKIN, J. S. *The Menomini Powwow*. Publications in Anthropology, vol. 4. Milwaukee: Milwaukee Public Museum, 1957. (A complete report on the Dream Dance religion in one typical tribe.)

SPIER, LESLIE, and SAPIR, EDWARD. *Wishram Ethnography*. Publications in Anthropology, vol. 5, no. 3. Seattle: University of Washington Press, 1930.

SWANTON, J. R. *Indians of the Southeastern United States*. Bulletin No. 137 of the Bureau of American Ethnology. Washington, D.C.: Smithsonian Institution, 1946.

TSCHOPIK, HARRY, JR. *Indians of North America*. New York: American Museum of Natural History, 1952. (A very good popular guide to the Indians north of Mexico.)

UNDERHILL, RUTH. *Pueblo Crafts*. Lawrence, Kans.: Haskell Institute, 1944.

VAILLANT GEORGE, C. *Indian Arts in North America*. New York: Harper & Bros., 1939.

WARDWELL, ALLEN. *Yakutat South: Indian Art of the Northwest Coast*. Chicago: Art Institute of Chicago, 1964.

WEST, GEORGE. *Tobacco Pipes and Smoking Customs of the American Indians*. 2 vols. Bulletin No. 17. Milwaukee: Milwaukee Public Museum, 1934.

WHITEFORD, ANDREW HUNTER. *North American Indian Arts*. New York: Golden Press, 1970.

WINGERT, PAUL S. *American Indian Sculptors*. New York: J. J. Augustin, 1949. (The sculpture of the southern part of the Northwest Coast, mainly Salish art.)

WISSLER, CLARK. *The American Indian*. New York: Oxford University Press, 1938.

———. *Indians of the United States*. New York: Doubleday, 1940.

List of Illustrations

29. Mask—Tsimshian (Kispiox, Gitksan, Upper Skeena River, B.C.)
30. Mask—Tsimshian (B.C.)
31. Shaman's charm—Tsimshian (probably of Niska origin but obtained from the Gitksan at Kitwangach, Skeena River, B.C.)
32. Ivory charm—Tsimshian
33. Ivory charm with pendants—Tsimshian (label states, "Haida–Skidegate")
34. Wooden trunk—Tlingit (Huna, Alaska)
35. Mask—Tlingit
36. Mask—Tlingit, Auk tribe (Pt. Lena, Alaska)
37. Face mask—Tlingit, Huna tribe (Chicagof Island)
38. Frontal mask—Tlingit
39. Maskette—Tlingit
40. Painted hide armor—Tlingit (Sitka, Alaska)
41. Stone mortar—Tlingit (?) (Alaska)
42. Carved puppet head—Haida (Skidegate, Queen Charlotte Islands, B.C.)
43. Carved puppet head—Haida (Skidegate, Queen Charlotte Islands, B.C.)
44. Opening mask—Haida
45. Wooden whistle with bellows—Haida
46. Medicine man's rattle—Haida (Clew, Queen Charlotte Islands, B.C.)
47. Shaman's dance rattle—Haida (Skidegate, Queen Charlotte Islands, B.C.)
48. Whistle-rattle—Haida (Skidegate, Queen Charlotte Islands, B.C.)
49. Small beaver bowl—Haida (Skidegate, Queen Charlotte Islands, B.C.)
50. Horn bowl—Haida
51. Horn bowl—Haida
52. Wooden pipe—Haida
53. Knife—Haida (possibly of Tlingit manufacture)
54. Mask—Eskimo (Lower Yukon, Alaska)
55. Mask—Eskimo (Pastolik, Alaska)
56. Mask—Eskimo (St. Michael, Norton Sound, Alaska)
57. Mask—Eskimo
58. Mask—Eskimo (Goodnews Bay)
59. Mask—Eskimo
60. Carved mask—Eskimo (Alaska), c. 1880
61. Mask—Eskimo (St. Michael, Norton Sound, Alaska)
62. Mask—Eskimo (Askeenick, near Cape Romanzoff, Alaska)
63. Mask—Eskimo (Norton Sound, Alaska)
64. Visor—Eskimo
65. Finger masks—Eskimo
66. Finger masks—Eskimo (Stebbins Island, off St. Michael, Norton Sound, Alaska; St. Michael, Norton Sound, Alaska; Rasbonsky, Alaska)
67. Doll—Eskimo (Diomede Island, Alaska)
68. Wooden figure—Eskimo (Kuskokwim River, Alaska)
69. Dance stick—Hunkpapa Sioux (Standing Rock Reservation, North Dakota)
70. Horse dance stick—Hunkpapa Sioux (Standing Rock Reservation, North Dakota)
71. Tomahawk Society wand—Arapaho
72. Human effigy wand (detail)—Assinaboin or Sioux (Ft. Peck)
73. Pipe bowl—Sioux (?) (Pipestone, Minnesota)
74. Tree-dweller doll—Santee Sioux
75. Tree-dweller doll—Santee Sioux
76. Mirror board—Omaha
77. Food bowl—Sisseton Sioux (North Dakota)
78. Wooden bowl in beaver form—tribe unknown (Great Lakes)
79. Wooden effigy bowl—Winnebago
80. Cow-horn spoons—Sioux
81. Cow-horn spoon—Sioux
82. War club—Iowa (Oklahoma)

83. Catlinite head of a war club—Sioux, 1900
84. Stone-headed war club (detail)—Sioux
85. War club—possibly Iroquois
86. Stone-headed war club (detail)—Sioux (Rosebud, South Dakota)
87. Rawhide rattle—Blackfoot (?), possibly Cheyenne (?)
88. Pipe and carved stem—Sioux, 1880–1900
89. Catlinite pipe bowl—probably Santee Sioux
90. Catlinite pipe bowl—Sioux (?)
91. Catlinite pipe bowl—possibly Sioux
92. Catlinite pipe bowl—Iowa (?)
93. Wood pipestem—Sioux (made at Ft. Snelling, 1833–36)
94. Shield—probably Arapaho (called Mandan by the Heye Foundation)
95. Wooden pipe bowl with stem—tribe unknown
96. Painted shield—Sioux
97. Pictographic painting—Sioux
98. Painted Ghost Dance shirt—Arapaho
99. Painted skin shirt—called Sauk but probably Santee Sioux
100. Pictographic drawing on paper—Sioux (Rosebud, South Dakota), c. 1890
101. Pictographic drawing on paper—Sioux (Rosebud, South Dakota), c. 1890
102. Kachina mask—Zuni
103. Buffalo fetish stone—Zuni
104. Stone bird fetish—Zuni
105. Altar carving—Zuni
106. War god—Zuni
107. Kachina doll—Zuni, Salimopia-Anahoho
108. Kachina doll—Zuni
109. Kachina doll—Zuni
110. Kachina doll—Hopi, Sio Calako
111. Kachina doll—Hopi
112. Double altar Kachina dolls—Hopi
113. Carving of a human figure—Hopi, c. 1870
114. Painted leather pouch and wooden doll—Apache
115. Painted cape—Chiricahua Apache
116. Clay figure—Cocopa (Lower California)
117. Clay doll—Mohave
118. Doll—Mohave
119. Doll with child—Mohave
120. Wood effigy—Klamath (Oregon)
121. Painted drum—Arapaho, 1890
122. Wooden pipe bowl (detail)—Ojibwa (White Earth Reservation, Minnesota)
123. Stone pipe bowl—Ojibwa (?)
124. Wooden pipe bowl with metal inlay—tribe unknown.
125. Pipe bowl of soapstone—tribe unknown (Great Lakes?)
126. Carved wooden head—Cree (Old Yellow Mill Trail, Manitoba)
127. Antler carving—Cree
128. Small ball-headed war club—Winnebago (Black River Falls, Wisconsin)
129. Wooden bowl in beaver form—Kaskaskia (?)
130. Small wooden bowl from Medicine Lodge—Winnebago (Sioux City, Iowa)
131. Mide doll—tribe unknown
132. Juggler dolls—Menominee
133. Mide doll—Ojibwa
134. Carved wooden doll—Ojibwa
135. Mide doll—Ojibwa (Berens River Band of Salteaux, Lake Winnipeg, Canada)
136. Stick rattle—Ojibwa
137. Love doll (male)—Prairie Potawatomi (Crandon, Wisconsin)
138. Mirror board (detail)—probably Woodland
139. Carved wooden heddle-frame—Fox (Tama, Iowa)
140. Crooked knife—Ojibwa (Beaver Island, Michigan)
141. False Face mask—Seneca (Cattaraugus

Reservation, New York) or possibly Tonawanda

142. False Face mask—Seneca (western New York)

143. Mask—Seneca (Cattaraugus Reservation, New York)

144. False Face mask—Iroquois (Grand River Reservation)

145. False Face mask—Iroquois (New York)

146. False Face mask—Iroquois (Six Nations Reservation, Grand River, Ontario)

147. Drumsticks—Delaware (Oklahoma)

148. Carved house post—Delaware (Big House near Copan, Oklahoma)

149. Carved house post with face on each side—Delaware (Copan, Oklahoma)

150. Carved wooden figure—Caddo